P9-DNL-492

31865002530094
641.563 BAU
The paleo kitchen : finding pr

the *paleo* kitchen

Finding Primal Joy in Modern Cooking

JU   BRYANT

4/15 9x

RIVER FOREST PUBLIC LIBRARY
735 Lathrop Avenue
River Forest, Illinois 60305
708 / 366-5205

8/14

First Published in 2014 by Victory Belt Publishing Inc.

Copyright © Juli Bauer and George Bryant

All rights reserved. No part of this publication may be reproduced or distributed in any form or by any means, electronic or mechanical, or stored in a database or retrieval system, without prior written permission from the publisher.

ISBN-13: 978-1-628600-10-0

This book is for entertainment purposes. The publisher and author of this cookbook are not responsible in any manner whatsoever for any adverse effects arising directly or indirectly as a result of the information provided in this book.

Printed in the USA

RRD 0314

Contents

Foreword

By Hayley Mason & Bill Staley
Bestselling authors of *Make It Paleo, Gather: The Art of Paleo Entertaining,* and *The 30-Day Guide to Paleo Cooking*

We fell in love with George and Juli the first time we met them, and yes, we said, "fell in love," because that's what happens to everyone who meets George and Juli: they fall in love with them. Their blogs have soared to the top in the Paleo community because these two charismatic individuals have won the heart of every one of their followers. Of course, part of their popularity can be attributed to their fabulous recipes, but it's also their humor and compassion that make them so darn likable. They are a Paleo cooking dream team, a powerhouse of delicious recipes, laughter, fun, play, and love. You can't help but smile when these two are in the room, and if you have the chance to see them cook together, you will walk away with a stomach sore from laughing.

We've been fortunate enough to watch George and Juli grow in the Paleo community, from starting their blogs to becoming immensely famous bloggers to, now, writing a cookbook together. The community would have been enthralled by the prospect of a cookbook written by either of them. How lucky are we that two of the brightest minds in Paleo teamed up to write one massive, incredibly beautiful, and well-thought-out cookbook? When they told us they were writing this book, we thought it was an absolutely brilliant idea, and we knew it would be a hit. From our first glance at the recipes, it was clear that assumption was completely correct. The inventive and unique recipes are accompanied by beautiful, drool-worthy photos. We even had a chance to taste some of the recipes from this book firsthand, cooked by George and Juli themselves! We can say without reservation that the recipes will knock your socks off, so make sure you eat these dishes barefoot.

The Paleo Kitchen offers the perfect recipes to help anyone start their own Paleo journey. Even better, they prove that Paleo cooking can be delicious and fun! The book contains all the tools needed to get started on the Paleo diet, without boring the Paleo veterans. And beyond all the helpful information and delectable recipes, the look and feel of this book will delight your senses. They say we eat with our eyes first. Put into terms that most Paleo advocates will appreciate, digestion truly starts with salivation. If these photos cause you to salivate, which they definitely will, then it could be hypothesized that cooking from this book will also promote good digestion!

George and Juli have outdone themselves with *The Paleo Kitchen*. This book has it all: great recipes, practical guides, and tons of useful information, all presented in the fun and approachable style that their regular blog readers know to expect. Whether you're just starting out or you're seeking new Paleo recipes, you will find what you're looking for in *The Paleo Kitchen*.

Paleo Stories

As the popularity of Paleo grows, more and more people are sharing the stories of how Paleo has changed their lives for the better. Even if you're new to Paleo, you have a story. Everyone does! It's your personal history with food and how your body reacts to certain foods. We hope you will try Paleo. If you do, you'll soon have your own story to share about its life-changing effects.

Juli's Story

JULI
BAUER

I've always loved food. But not just any kind of food. Mostly packaged cookies, lasagna from the freezer section, frosting (lots of frosting), and packaged cookies dipped in frosting. Of course. I mean, why wouldn't you dip sugar into sugar? Real food that came from the ground and the earth around us wasn't in my vocabulary. All I knew was what came from a factory. I hated all vegetables, I didn't really like meat, and I had absolutely no understanding of the importance of food. I knew that packaged food made me happy, and I knew that I was addicted to it. When I think back to my eating habits, I honestly don't think I knew what hunger felt like. I would eat out of boredom, eat because I was depressed, eat because I was happy. I was just constantly eating. I was, hands down, addicted to food. And, even more so, to sugar.

But over time, packaged foods and their overwhelming amounts of sugar began to work against me. I was haunted by digestive issues and intense stomach pains that landed me in the emergency room. But there was no real diagnosis for these issues, and not once did my doctor ask me about what I was eating. Even with my constant weight fluctuations, the only thing my doctor ever asked was if I was taking vitamins—not if I was getting vitamins from my food. So I never even wondered if the food I was eating was good for me.

It wasn't until my senior year of college in 2010 that I began to question what I ate. I had a boyfriend at the time who ate an incredibly strict diet and looked the part. He introduced me to CrossFit, and that was when my life completely changed. I had always enjoyed working out, mostly because it made me feel more confident, but I was plagued with body issues and body dysmorphia. Even though I loved working out, it was always for the wrong reason: to be as thin as possible. I never thought about being as fit as possible. After trying one CrossFit workout with my boyfriend, which included burpees, I gave up immediately. It was unlike any workout I had ever tried. So I took on modified CrossFit workouts on my own. I found workouts all over the Internet and adjusted them to what I could do. I did push-ups on my knees, assisted machine pull-ups, and squats with just the barbell. The more I did CrossFit, the more I fell in love with it because of the results I was seeing. Not only did I look different, but I was able to improve on a daily basis. Before I knew it, I was doing push-ups on my toes and unassisted pull-ups, and I could squat more than I ever thought possible. All I wanted to do was improve: improve in the gym, improve my life, and improve my diet. CrossFit showed me that I was a strong woman who did not have to be plagued by body issues and self-hatred. It proved to me that anything was possible.

The more I did CrossFit, the more I was hooked. And once I joined a CrossFit affiliate, I knew that I absolutely wanted to compete in CrossFit. That's when diet became a key factor in my life. I was never the strongest in the gym and never the fastest, but I knew that if I could control what I put into my body, I would keep myself the healthiest during competitions. So, as I trained for competitions, I slowly began to remove unneeded carbohydrates and refined grains from my diet, cookie by cookie. It was not an easy thing at the beginning, especially since I was so addicted to sugar. But over time, all my stomach issues went away, along with my depression, self-hatred towards my body, poor sleep, and lack of energy. Even though I loved eating those fake foods so much, I loved the results of giving them up even more: I had never felt better or more confident in my life, and I didn't want to lose that.

Over a six- to nine-month period, I removed all processed and packaged foods from my diet and went completely Paleo. And because of that, my performance in the gym got better and better. I became dedicated to my daily routine at the gym in hopes of making it to the 2011 CrossFit Southwest Regional. And that's what I did. I finished eleventh overall in the region and went back in 2012 to finish eighth overall. And I owe a good percentage of that performance to my eating habits. Eating the right foods—real foods—helped me to be stronger and faster. I ate the foods that are made for our bodies and that help us thrive.

After eating Paleo for a few months, I began to love cooking. I had never really cooked much before, and when I had, I had failed miserably. (Now I know that it's much harder to get good results in the kitchen with fake food than real food.) I realized that if I was ever going to stick with Paleo, I had to master cooking and actually enjoy it. So I began to cook recipes from blogs, take pictures of the food, and share those pictures on my gym's website. Before I knew it, I was creating my own recipes and absolutely loved it. Making delicious food was such a satisfying

Juli at the CrossFit Southwest Regional in 2011

feeling. So, to share those recipes with as many people as possible, I created my own blog: paleomg.com.

My blog started off very small, just one or two recipes a week with absolutely terrible camera-phone pictures. At that time, I was working at four CrossFit gyms, so I took pictures at 4:30 a.m. as I headed out for the day or at 10:00 p.m. when I got home. I didn't have much time to dedicate to my blog, but I loved it. The more I began to share stories of my love life and life in the gym, the more comments began to roll in, not only about the recipes, but also about my stories. People actually enjoyed my blunt and honest humor. So I began to incorporate stories into every recipe post, and before I knew it, my blog began to take off. I began receiving emails from people thanking me for my blog. I had never set out to change people's lives through food or through my journaling, but that's what happened. Because of that, I continued to create recipes and share my life stories.

The biggest thing I have learned from creating my blog is that a diet can actually be quite a positive experience, especially when it's not about limiting calories but about eating real food. The Paleo diet has taught me that life is about living the best life possible. A diet does not have to be about restrictions; it can be about possibilities. I've tailored the Paleo diet to my needs and to my lifestyle. I take an 80/20 approach—I eat as Paleo as possible 80 percent of the time and enjoy my life the rest of it. That 20 percent leeway gives me the opportunity to have fun at the parties I go to and enjoy the special moments in life with a gluten-free cookie or piece of wedding cake. Life is all about balance, and through CrossFit and Paleo, I've found my balance.

CrossFit and Paleo have led me to where I am today, creating multiple recipes every week for any person who comes across my blog. I want Paleo to feel lighthearted and keep people from ever feeling deprived when it comes to food. Options are what keep people eating Paleo—which is why George and I came together to create this cookbook. This cookbook brings together different cooking styles and ideas from George and me, all in the hopes of keeping you full and satisfied with every meal you create.

George's Story

GEORGE
BRYANT

I am so excited to be able to share with you a few of the many reasons why I chose the Paleo lifestyle. I really want you to be able to understand my journey, and I hope it will help you along yours. When I began my new lifestyle, I did not—and still do not—want to be dogmatic; I don't believe that there is a one-size-fits-all approach or that there is always one answer. The beautiful thing about life is that we get to make our own decisions and live out the results. Sometimes we learn lessons, sometimes we make mistakes, and other times, we just land smack down on the pavement. No matter what the result, we keep pressing forward and molding ourselves into who we want to become.

I want to remind you of this because all too often, I see people fall off the "diet" train. Maybe they eat some fruit during a sugar detox or ingest some seed oils while eating dinner with friends, and then they become discouraged. What we need is to create positive spaces for ourselves in order to thrive, and that starts with loving ourselves for who we are, as well as for the choices we have made. When you fall, stand up, brush yourself off, and take a step forward. You already fell down. You can't go back and prevent it from happening, so there is no reason to worry about it—just learn your lesson and try your best to prevent it from happening again. There are already enough negative and judgmental people and things in this world. Let's not add to the pile when it comes to self-reflection.

The reason I choose to share my views on self-reflection and positive thinking is that I spent the majority of my life doing everything but thinking positive. I have always been my own worst enemy. I allowed myself at a very young age to become a victim of my circumstances, and it has taken me fifteen years and many speed bumps to get to where I am today. These speed bumps have taught me life lessons that I now share through my food and lifestyle choices. The most important life lesson of them all has been loving and accepting myself.

Early in my childhood, I struggled with weight problems and developed a very unhealthy body image. I spent the majority of my life overweight and completely out of shape. I tried participating in sports while I was in high school, but the combination of bullying, lack of drive, and lack of guidance stood in my way. I came from an unstable home environment where family meals were unheard of, and, as a result, fast food made up most of my diet. My lack of physical activity, unhealthy eating habits, and lack of knowledge and support from others led me down a very long and dark road. This was the road of disordered eating, which eventually, thankfully, led me to a way to become truly happy and healthy.

The first time I can remember ever wanting to learn how to get in shape or make a huge change in my life was when I attempted to join the Marine Corps.

During my first attempt to enlist in the Marines, the recruiters took one look at me, put me on the scale, and told me I was forty-three pounds overweight. If I wanted to enlist, I was going to need to lose that weight. Being a stubborn, misguided, and scared young man, I made it my mission to prove those recruiters wrong. I started reading, researching, running, working out like a fiend, and attacking the excess weight with whatever information I could find. The pounds certainly did not melt away. I was overworking my body and myself, undereating, and basically setting myself up for failure. After extensive struggling, my disordered eating took over. I would go for long periods without eating at all, and I would purge after my meals. I was doing all this while being extremely orthorexic and continuing my unhealthy and extensive workouts.

It took four months for me to lose the extra weight. This was weight I pretended had come off in an efficient and healthy manner. However, the truth was that I was a seventeen-year-old boy who was desperately trying to hide his insecurities; looking back now, I know that overcompensating in actions and words was my attempt to do just that. I walked

George
during his
Marine Corps
days in 2011
↓

back into the recruiter's office looking, on the face of it, as if I had made an amazing self-transformation. I proceeded to sign the papers and began my path in the Marine Corps.

After I advanced as an Honor Graduate from Parris Island in 2002, I weighed a mere 154 pounds and was constantly engaged in work and training. Being that busy and skinny turned out to be a great Band-Aid for my insecurities; it allowed me a respite from my struggle with bulimia. It wasn't until I was deployed to Somalia in 2004 that my unhealthy obsession with overcompensating to hide my secrets spun completely out of control. I kept myself busy with my need to fill downtime while deployed, hiding my disordered eating and hatred for my body. This turned into an obsession with getting as big and strong as humanly possible. My thought process became this: "If I lift extreme amounts of weight, look strong, and have a small waist, somehow I will love myself because then I will be perfect." This led ultimately to my weighing in at a solid 253 pounds: a hulking weight for a guy only 5 feet 7 inches tall.

The bubble of glory and false comfort I had created for myself was short-lived. To put it simply, someone my size is not supposed to weigh that much. Between the stresses I put on myself from my workouts, USMC forced marches with fully loaded rucksacks, and distance runs, I was overworked and completely exhausted. It was too much for my body to handle, and I developed exercise-induced compartment syndrome, which caused me to nearly lose both of my legs. Now, let's fast-forward through five operations I underwent.

George running the Niketown 30k in Honolulu ↓

I spent the majority of a year in a wheelchair. All that muscle I had worked so hard to build? It was now turning into fat. Several months of eating hospital food, popping pain pills, and doing wheelchair "exercises" took their toll on me. It became clear that I would be kicked out of the military if I couldn't regain strength— it was either shape up or ship out. At the same time, I got very negative news from the doctors: I would never run again—even walking would be difficult—and lifting weights was completely out of the question. It wasn't until I heard "you can't" again that I knew I could, and would, prove them wrong in order to keep my bulimia a secret.

After showing some improvement, I was transferred to Hawaii, where I was blessed to receive some excellent physical therapy. Soon after, I was introduced to a new obsession: triathlons. Three years of training and racing in Hawaii dropped my weight down to 178 pounds, but I was skinny-fat. I looked great in clothes, but underneath I looked like I had never done a workout in my life. I wasn't truly fit.

In August 2010, I started CrossFit while deployed in Afghanistan, and everything changed. I spent seven months throwing myself *into the WOD-style challenges of CrossFit and adopting a Paleo lifestyle as best I could with the chow-hall food. After my deployment in Afghanistan ended in 2011, I returned to California. This was the time when I started to become more serious about Paleo, and I attempted to teach myself how to cook. I started my website, civilizedcavemancooking.com, to have a place to post recipes in order to hold myself accountable. Since then, my site has created an amazing community of supportive people, all of whom are discovering their journeys in the food and health communities.*

Throughout my journey of creating recipes, learning food photography and website design, and the other 342 jobs that come with running a website, I found my health and, most importantly, the love I have for myself. I am not Paleo-perfect, nor do I strive to be. Grain-free cookies and chocolate simply taste too delicious. Instead, I eat foods that nourish my body and make me feel good, and I do so while avoiding things that upset my tummy. My website has become a place for me to share those easy and delicious creations, and it has served as proof that having fun in the kitchen and loving yourself is the best place to start on any health journey.

Here I am today, at the close of fifteen years of self-reflection and speed bumps. I am a brand-new person, and I am completely in love with life. I love my body, food, my life, and myself. Due to certain lingering injuries from deployments, I have been medically separated from the Marine Corps. Now I am attacking the blogging world full-time. This recent shift in my life has allowed me to embark on another new journey. I have been granted the opportunity to create this cookbook with my amazing friend, Juli. My goal is to share with you all the fun I am able to have in the kitchen. My hopes are that you can replicate this fun in your home and make cooking something you look forward to every day. (I would include eating as something to look forward to as well, but I know we all love eating enough already.) Working with Juli has created an entire new avenue of creativity and flavors I never knew were possible. She truly is a food genius, and I look forward to sharing all our creations with you.

The Story
of This Book

We come from different backgrounds and different experiences, but Paleo brought us together. After starting our blogs within the same month about three years ago, we began following each other's blogs and re-creating each other's recipes. Before we knew it, we were chatting online about recipes and how to improve our blogs.

For two years, we stayed in contact through email, Facebook, and text messages while sharing recipe ideas and helping each other troubleshoot our websites. We re-created each other's recipes, sometimes with our own unique spins, and shared them with our communities to help promote each other.

While in the planning stages for the annual three-day PaleoFX conference in Austin, Texas, we decided that we should do a cooking demonstration together. We had never met and never cooked together, but we decided it would be a great idea to do it for the first time in front of a live audience. After playing email tag we came up with a recipe that neither of us had made before and decided to just go with it. We ended up having a blast cooking together, and the recipe was amazing. Best of all, the audience was cracking up, and we even laughed at ourselves a few times.

During that weekend in Texas, we met our publisher, Erich Krauss at Victory Belt, and began contemplating writing a book together. All we really knew about each other was that we enjoyed the same food and the same friends. Besides our one-off cooking demo at the conference, we knew nothing about working together or creating a project together, but we decided to take the plunge anyway and signed a book deal.

Before we knew it, Juli was flying out to California multiple times each month to work on the cookbook with George. It took around seven or eight trips to get all the recipes done. The first trip was probably the hardest. It was the first time we really began to get to know each other and see each other's at-home habits—like how George likes to clean as he goes while Juli likes to let the kitchen explode, or how George keeps every cabinet open while Juli follows behind him to close them all. It just so happened that during that first getting-to-know-each-other's-work-habits trip, we were creating the dessert recipes for the book. Eating only sweets for a week straight while dealing with a new roommate . . . it can be challenging. After we got out of our sugar coma and started to understand each other's recipe development and cooking style more, our creativity was unstoppable, and we continued to create delicious recipes, one after another. Not all of our recipes came out perfectly. We had plenty of recipes that failed. We would pout for a couple hours and then go back to testing the recipe. Our cinnamon rolls, for instance—we're pretty sure we tried that recipe a good three times before it came out perfectly.

THANKFULLY, ALL YOU HAVE TO DO NOW IS ENJOY THE PERFECTED RECIPES.

What Is Paleo?
And Is It Right for You?

Seeing as how Paleo was the most Googled diet of 2013, there are a lot more people finding out about it. People call it "Paleo," "Primal," "Paleolithic," or even the "Caveman Diet." Let us make a few things clear first: 1) this is not a diet; and 2) we are not cavemen and cavewomen. We do not live in caves, we are not being chased by saber-toothed tigers, and we all use twenty-first-century technology in one way or another. "Paleo," "Primal," and "Paleolithic" are just names that are used to refer to the way we choose to eat. It is safe to say that we do not need to act like cavepeople in order to live this lifestyle.

I MEAN, CAN YOU ENVISION WALKING INTO YOUR OFFICE AND SEEING EVERYONE DRESSED IN LOINCLOTHS? GROSS. NO, THANK YOU.

Since we don't plan to act like cavepeople, we also won't eat exactly like them. Even though Paleo is considered the "caveman diet," it is actually more of a template to help you choose what foods to put into your body to allow your body to heal and thrive.

The whole idea of Paleo is quite simple: by eating foods that nourish your body and allow chronic inflammation to subside and heal, you can create a path to let your body start thriving instead of just surviving. You don't need to have food allergies in order to try eating Paleo. We think it is important for everyone to try Paleo, even if you don't experience adverse side effects from eating processed foods. Why wait until you're feeling unhealthy to try Paleo? Why just feel okay when you can feel great? If you're anything like the thousands before you who have made the transition to Paleo, you will experience positive benefits you didn't know were possible.

So don't be scared to try Paleo. Why not try something new if it will leave you looking and feeling so much better? We all absorb nutrients and vitamins in different ways. If there is a new lifestyle that will elevate your mood and make your body look and feel better, why not try it?

Many people turn to Paleo because they have confirmed food allergies or are symptomatic and think they may be allergic to certain foods. If that describes you, you can use Paleo to create a diet that's customized for your needs. If you think you may have allergies, we strongly recommend you omit complete food groups from your diet for an allotted time period (usually a minimum of thirty days is recommended). Start with grains, proceed to refined sugar, and then go on to dairy. Taking small steps, such as removing the bread from sandwiches or swapping apple slices and almond butter for your normal crackers and peanut butter, will get you onto a healthier path. Once you begin to make these small steps, keep a close eye on how your body reacts: Take a look at your skin, hair, and gut. Watch how your sleeping patterns change and improve. Pay attention to your energy levels throughout the day. With these observations, you'll be able to figure out which food groups may harm your mind and body. According to your results, you can omit certain food groups if you deem it necessary and healthy for you.

FOR MORE INFORMATION ON REMOVING FOODS FROM YOUR DIET, TURN TO "GETTING TO KNOW YOUR BODY," PAGE 24.

Read, Cook, Create, and Love Paleo

One of the great things about Paleo is that there are tons of resources out there—blogs, books, and passionate Paleo people (like us) who are happy to share their positive stories and give supportive advice. If you want to do a bit more research before committing to a Paleo lifestyle, do as we did: we both started by figuring out the science behind Paleo and why it was so beneficial. So check out some of the scientific reads out there and then start cooking—not only from this cookbook but also from some of the amazing food blogs out there! In the back of this book, we've included a list of impressive authors who cover the scientific aspects of Paleo and a list of our favorite Paleo cooking blogs. But don't restrict yourself to this list. Paleo is such a hot topic that by the time this book hits bookstore shelves, there will probably be another half dozen great Paleo cooking blogs out there.

With this cookbook, we hope to bring diversity to your meals and keep you from ever feeling deprived or bored. We've created simple recipes with ingredients that will keep your taste buds happy and energy levels high. These foods range from simple breakfast ideas to fancier weekend meals. But all of them will bring back memories: from childhood Sunday morning pancakes and Friday night burgers to your favorite Chinese restaurant meal, Grandma's famous Italian meatballs, and chocolate brownies. We created this cookbook so that you can eat healthy, good-for-you meals that are reminiscent of the comfort foods you grew up eating or have come to love. Going Paleo is a whole lot easier when you discover you don't have to leave behind all those good memories and happy emotions that are associated with your favorite foods. With our recipes, you get to re-experience them in healthy Paleo versions.

NOW ALL YOU HAVE TO DO IS TAKE THE FIRST STEP.

Let's Get Started

In this section, you'll find out how to get started on your Paleo body makeover and Paleo kitchen makeover. The first steps in getting started on your new Paleo lifestyle are all about eliminating and replenishing: out with the bag of chips, in with the organic produce. It's all about getting to know your own body better and getting yourself into a new frame of mind with a new set of habits. We've thrown in some tips to help you get going on your own Paleo journey and form some new Paleo habits of your own.

Getting to Know Your Body

Paleo can help you understand your body and its needs, making it easy to create a diet of nourishing foods that is customized to your needs.

During the first thirty days of your new Paleo lifestyle, abstain from all foods that are on the "avoid" list at right. This will allow chronic inflammation to heal and the gut to repair itself. Then gradually reintroduce starchy vegetables, dairy products, and alcohol one at a time and observe how your body reacts. During this period of reintroduction, you may determine that you have a food intolerance. This is particularly common with dairy. Most people discover that once they've transitioned to Paleo and removed dairy from their lifestyle, they can no longer tolerate dairy. If you can tolerate dairy, however, we urge you to only use raw whole milk, cream, and grass-fed butter to ensure your body is getting the freshest and most nutritious food. Conventionally processed dairy from nonpastured animals should be avoided. Many find that they cannot tolerate alcohol at all; others find that just avoiding grain-based alcohol makes a huge difference.

PALEO IS ALSO A GREAT WAY TO EXPLORE HOW YOUR BODY REACTS TO DIFFERENT TYPES OF RED AND WHITE MEAT, SEAFOOD, AND FISH.

Depending on your genetics, you will likely harbor diverse physical reactions to eating different varieties of meat and seafood.

You have a wide variety of meat to choose from when eating Paleo: white meat, red meat, game meat, and more. If you don't like to eat red meat, try chicken breast, ground turkey, and other poultry.

If you don't like the rich and fishy taste of salmon, stick to white fish, such as tilapia, swai, and cod.

A PALEO CHECKLIST

HERE IS A SNAPSHOT OF
WHAT YOU SHOULD BE
EATING ON A DAILY BASIS:

GRASS-FED MEATS

WILD-CAUGHT FISH
AND SEAFOOD

VEGETABLES — particularly
leafy greens and
other low-starch
vegetables

FRUITS

NUTS and SEEDS

HEALTHY FATS/OILS

including
corn and soy

all processed foods
or foods with long,
indecipherable
ingredients lists

AND THE FOODS
YOU SHOULD AVOID:

ABSOLUTELY ALL GRAINS

"FAKE FOOD"

REFINED OILS and SUGARS

LEGUMES

STARCHY VEGETABLES,
PARTICULARLY WHITE
POTATOES*

DAIRY*

ALCOHOL*

* YOU CAN REINTRODUCE
STARCHY VEGETABLES, DAIRY,
AND ALCOHOL TO YOUR DIET
AFTER THE FIRST THIRTY DAYS
OF THE TRANSITION PERIOD
TO DETERMINE IF YOU HAVE
SENSITIVITIES TO THEM.

Tips for Getting Started on Your Paleo Journey

Get yourself that one kitchen gadget you have been eyeing for months.

This could be anything from a new set of tableware to a high-end blender to an espresso machine. Believe it or not, this may be all it takes for you to want to start spending more time in the kitchen!

BUY IT AND SMILE

Go through all your cabinets.

Free up all that space! If you have extra pots and pans or more than two sets of flatware and dishware, put the extra into storage. It will be accessible if you absolutely need it, but you will also be able to utilize that space better once you begin cooking.

Try to make your kitchen a fun place to spend time.

One of the very first things you could do is set up a Bluetooth docking station for your cell phone. Blasting music while cooking is always fun. You can sing, dance, and jump around in the process.

Just don't dance too much while frying bacon—grease burns hurt.

Bring your kids into the kitchen.

The more your kids help cook their own food, the better they will understand what they are eating and why. When you have the whole family on board with eating Paleo, the transition will be much easier.

Learn to shop and cook smartly.

We have lots of tips to help you with this on pages 45 to 59.

Figure out what your staple items are going to be and then decide on the best spot for each of them to reside.

Anything you will be using on a daily basis (such as cooking oil, spices, herbs, fresh vegetables, and meat) should be kept someplace easy to access. Keep veggies and meat in the front of the refrigerator, and put herbs within easy reach from where you will be cooking at your stovetop.

Decide what your bulk items are going to be.

Figure out if it would be best to buy these items online in bulk quantities or from the bulk section of your local grocery store. Buy some storage containers for bulk items; plastic bags can be too easily pierced or ripped and create a mess.

Decide with your family how often you will be going out to eat and how much time you will spend preparing and eating meals at home.

That way you can accurately determine how much time you will need to spend cooking throughout the week, and there will be less food wasted.

Also, you will get a better idea of how many storage containers you will need to purchase.

If you are going to incorporate a new workout program into your new lifestyle as well, make sure you are eating enough throughout the day.

One of the biggest mistakes you can make when adapting to the Paleo lifestyle and working out is not eating enough calories throughout the day. How are you going to get through that intense, hour-long workout if all you've had to eat all day is that morning coffee and a few eggs? Keep your body filled with nutrients and enough food to give you some power throughout your workout.

Get support from friends and family.

Let them know you will be exploring a new lifestyle. Yeah, they may make fun of you and give you a hard time at first, but give them fair warning. That way, the next time you all gather for a family celebration, your great-aunt will not be offended if you reject her third offer in a row for that peach cobbler. Your family and friends *love* you. If you are taking a step to try and better yourself, they will do their best to support you, we are sure.

Figure out what your favorite types of food are.

What kinds of food do you truly *enjoy*? You can come full-circle and re-create some of those favorites with healthier Paleo recipes. If you love carrot cake and pizza, we promise you that there are recipes out there in the blogosphere that you can use to create more nutrient-dense and better versions of those favorite foods.

One bad meal isn't going to ruin your progress, and one good meal surely will not make you healthy.

Don't completely resist something you have been craving. Chances are, if you are craving something, you will continue to crave it until you satisfy that craving in some way. Figure out what your cravings are and how to fix them.

YOU'LL BE MUCH HAPPIER, HEALTHIER, AND, OH YEAH, SANE!

Ask for guidance.

The Paleo community is a very happy and friendly community overall. If you have a question about a recipe on a blog, chances are someone else has had that question before. Scroll through the comments section and see if you can find an answer. Most bloggers tend to be pretty good about answering their readers' questions. And if they haven't answered it, another reader may have! You can talk to George directly on his website at civilizedcavemancooking.com or to Juli at paleomg.com.

IF YOU HAVE MORE SPECIFIC QUESTIONS, YOU CAN FIND OUR EMAIL ADDRESSES ON OUR WEBSITES.

The Paleo Kitchen Makeover

The sometimes-daunting first step is the hardest, but taking that step will be one of the best decisions you've made. And even though it may seem harder in the beginning, eating Paleo and creating Paleo-inspired meals becomes easier the more you do it. So let's take the first step: clear out the pantry!

You are going to find cans of beans that have been expired since the new millennium, Oreos, jars of peanut butter, and maybe even some Fruit Roll-Ups or Capri Sun. Don't throw this stuff in the trash, but get rid of it. Donate it to a local shelter or give it to a friend or neighbor. You want it out of sight, because out of sight means out of mind.

From the pantry, move on to the refrigerator and freezer, removing dairy products, condiments with high fructose corn syrup, meats with additives that you can't pronounce, frozen dinners, and anything else with ingredients you're unsure of. Remember, you are trying to get back to simple eating. If a product has a huge ingredients list, you don't want it in your house. An apple doesn't have an ingredient list on it for a reason. Stick with simple foods.

Once you've taken the first step on your Paleo journey and cleared out your pantry, fridge, and freezer of all fake foods, especially those that are on the "avoid" list (see the sidebar on page 25), you can restock your fridge and pantry with real foods and your Paleo journey can begin.

Buy organic fruits and vegetables as much as possible, and buy what is in season. You will get better-quality produce and save money by visiting local farmers markets. And try to eat nonstarchy vegetables more often than not. We enjoy sweet potatoes, winter squash, and root vegetables on occasion.

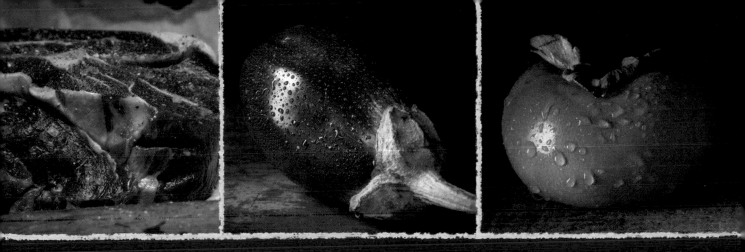

Meats, Veggies, and Fruits

These are the foods you will need to purchase on a regular basis. They make up the bulk of what you'll be eating, so whenever possible, buy quality meats and produce.

When buying meat, poultry, seafood, and fish, remember that grass-fed, pastured, and wild-caught are the best choices. Try to eat local and know where your meat is being sourced from. The list that follows is a snapshot of popular choices; don't feel you need to restrict yourself to it. There are plenty of other options: duck, rabbit, goat, and more.

PROTEINS

Beef

Bison

Chicken

Eggs

Fish and seafood of all types, including shellfish

venison, elk, etc. → Game

High-quality cured meats (charcuterie/salumi)

Lamb

Organ meats ← liver, heart, etc.

Pork

bacon, pancetta, prosciutto, dry cured sausage, etc.

Smoked fish and shellfish, such as salmon and oysters

Turkey ← FRESH AND SMOKED

FRUITS

Fall

Apples

Cranberries

Figs

Grapes

Limes

Melons

Pears

Persimmons

Pomegranates

Winter

Clementines

Grapefruit

Kiwi

Kumquats

Mandarins

NAVEL → Oranges

Persimmons

Pomelos

Tangerines

NAVEL and VALENCIA

Spring

Apricots ← LATE SPRING

Cherries

Grapefruit

Kiwi

Kumquats

Oranges

Rhubarb

Strawberries

Summer

Apples

Avocados

SUMMER BUT HARVESTED YEAR-ROUND

Blackberries

Blueberries

Boysenberries ← late summer

Cantaloupe ← early summer

Cherries

Figs

Gooseberries

Grapes

Limes

Mangoes

Melons

Nectarines

Oranges ← VALENCIA

Peaches

Plums and pluots

Raspberries

Rhubarb

Strawberries

Watermelons

VEGGIES

31

LET'S GET
STARTED

Fall

Artichokes
Arugula
Beets
Brussels sprouts
Cabbage
Cauliflower
Celery
Celery root
Chard
Eggplant
Endives
Escarole *fall through spring*
Fennel *fall through spring*
Garlic
Green beans
Jerusalem artichokes
Kale *late fall through spring*
Kohlrabi
Leeks *FALL THROUGH SPRING*
Okra
Parsnips
Peppers *SUMMER and EARLY FALL*
Pumpkins
Shallots *SUMMER AND FALL*
Sweet potatoes
Turnips *FALL AND WINTER*
FALL THROUGH SPRING

Winter

Beets *fall through spring*
Bok choy
Brussels sprouts
Cabbage
Cauliflower
Celery
Celery root
Endives
Escarole
Jerusalem artichokes
Kale
Squash *FALL AND WINTER*
Sweet potatoes

Spring

Artichokes
Arugula
Asparagus
Beets
Green onions *spring through fall*
Onions
Pea greens
Peas *SPRING and EARLY SUMMER*
Radishes
Scallions *spring through fall*
Snap peas

Summer

Beets
Chard
Chiles
Cucumbers
Eggplant
Garlic
Green beans
Okra *spring and early summer*
Peas
Peppers *SUMMER AND EARLY FALL*
Radicchio *late summer*
Shallots
Squash *SUMMER AND FALL*
Tomatillos
Tomatoes *LATE SUMMER, EARLY FALL*
Zucchini

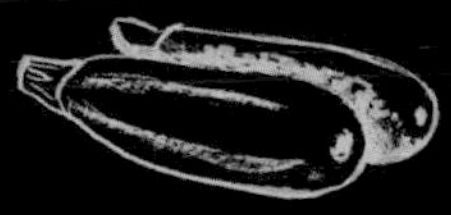

Year-Round

Broccoli *YEAR-ROUND BUT BEST IN FALL AND WINTER*
Carrots
Collard greens
Lettuce
Mushrooms
Spinach
Sprouts
Various herbs

Nonperishables

These are the foods you will need to purchase every so often. Some of these items are best stored at room temperature, in airtight containers, in a cupboard (or other dark spots away from light). Some do best in the refrigerator or freezer for longer keeping times.

NUTS AND SEEDS

Almond butter and other nut
butters (cashew, macadamia,
sunflower seed, etc.)

Almond meal/flour

*For a longer
shelf life, store in
the refrigerator*

Almonds

Cashews

Macadamia nuts

Pecans

Pistachios

*For a longer
shelf life,
store in the
freezer*

HEALTHY COOKING FATS

Avocado oil

Bacon fat

Coconut oil

Duck fat

Ghee

Grass-fed butter

Lard

Macadamia nut oil

Olive oil

Optional: Extra virgin olive oil

Tallow

Walnut oil

*CHECK LABELS
TO SEE IF THESE
SHOULD BE
STORED IN THE
REFRIGERATOR*

if you do dairy

*FOR
COOKING*

*FOR USE AS A
FINISHING OIL
AND IN SALAD
DRESSINGS*

BAKING NEEDS

Arrowroot powder

Baking powder

Baking soda

Blanched almond meal/flour

Coconut butter

Coconut flour

Coconut milk,
full fat (canned)

Coconut oil

Coconut sugar

Dark chocolate

Lemon extract

Nut flours

Poppy seeds

Tapioca flour

Unsweetened and
unsulfured dried fruit

Unsweetened cocoa powder

Unsweetened coconut flakes

Unsweetened shredded coconut

Vanilla extract

Whole vanilla beans

*we prefer
almond flour
from Honeyville*

*also known as
coconut cream
concentrate*

*We like Enjoy Life
Mini Chocolate Chips
and Mega Chunks or
72-percent cacao baking
chocolate from Eating
Evolved.*

NATURAL SWEETENERS

Organic honey

Coconut sugar

Maple sugar

Maple syrup

Dried fruits ← *NO SUGAR ADDED*

Blackstrap molasses

Pitted dates

use Grade B for more maple flavor (ideal for baking) and Grade A (fancy) when you want less maple flavor (to sweeten tea, for example)

FOR FLAVOR
(some for the pantry, some for the fridge)

Coconut aminos

Dijon mustard

Extracts: vanilla and lemon

Homemade mayo, plain and flavored (page 290)

Homemade ketchup (page 291)

Homemade pesto (page 293)

Hot sauce

Sesame oil

Sesame seeds

Stone-ground mustard

Vinegars ← *BALSAMIC AND APPLE CIDER*

Yellow mustard

SPICES, HERBS, AROMATICS, AND SALT (most used)

Allspice, ground

Basil leaves ← *FRESH AND DRIED*

Bay leaf

Black pepper

Cayenne pepper

Chili powder

Chives ←

Cilantro ← *FRESH*

Cinnamon, sticks and ground

Cloves, ground

Coriander, ground

Curry powder

Dill ← *FRESH*

Fennel fronds

Garlic powder

Garlic ←

Ginger ← *FRESH*

Ginger, ground

Mint ← *FRESH*

Nutmeg

Onion powder

Oregano, dried ground

Parsley

fresh and dried

Red pepper flakes

Rosemary ← *FRESH AND DRIED*

Sage ←

Sea salt ← *COARSE AND FINE-GRAIN*

Smoked paprika

Tarragon ← *FRESH*

Thyme leaves ←

White pepper

FRESH AND DRIED

CANNED, JARRED, OR BOXED FOODS

Canned coconut milk and cream

Canned fish

Canned fruit ← SUGAR- AND CORN SYRUP-FREE

Canned tomatoes

Coconut water

Pumpkin puree

Stock ←

Sun-dried tomatoes — BEEF, PORK, CHICKEN, VEGETABLE

Tomato paste

Tomato sauce

Kitchen Tools & Equipment

Having the right tools and equipment will make your food preparation not only easier but also more enjoyable. When adopting a Paleo lifestyle, which entails cooking with whole, unprocessed ingredients, you have to learn how to prepare food from scratch. No more packaged dinners, take-out nights, or simply heating a bag of food in a pan of water. For some people that may be stressful, so we want to make it as simple as possible. Having tools that enable you to be more efficient, and enjoy the process, is a good thing. We all love getting new toys—now you have an excuse to spoil yourself a little more.

The Top Ten

We don't expect you to buy all the tools we mention, and certainly not all at once. So we'll start with the top ten that will help you make most of our recipes with ease.

Quality knives & knife sharpener

Make your life easier by investing in good knives and keeping them sharpened. They will help you create the exact cut you want with your foods, and when they're kept sharp, they are safer to use than dull knives. You don't need a full block of knives that you will never use; one good chef's knife and a paring knife will cover almost all of your needs. To keep your knives sharp, you will need a knife sharpener (we recommend a whetstone) and a honing steel. You can buy a manual knife sharpener, rods, or sharpening stone for a very affordable price online or in stores.

See page 59 for some general guidance on maintaining a sharp blade.

Cast-iron skillets

We love using well-seasoned cast-iron skillets. For the recipes in this book, you will need a medium (10-inch/25-cm) skillet and a large (12-inch/30-cm) skillet. Never use soap when washing your cast-iron skillets. After cooking, use hot water and a clean sponge to remove any food remnants. Once clean, hand-dry the pan and lightly coat it with coconut oil to maintain its nonstick surface. The longer you continue to season your cast-iron pan, the more nonstick the surface will become.

A food processor will pay for itself before you know it, and your wrists will thank you over and over again.

Cutting boards

Invest in a good wooden cutting board, especially if you want to save those sharp knives you invested in. Wooden cutting boards absorb the force of the cut, so they won't dull your knives. Ceramic, plastic, and glass cutting boards dull your knives and decrease the life of your blades. Plus, plastic cutting boards can harbor as much bacteria as wooden ones, if not more—so toss that idea out of your head.

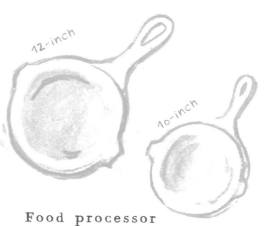

12-inch

10-inch

Food processor

Perfect for flawlessly slicing and chopping vegetables; grinding nuts, seeds, and meat; shredding and pureeing; and mixing and kneading dough, a food processor is the biggest time-saver. We used a Magimix 16-cup food processor for mega recipe-testing workouts for this book, but a 7- or 9-cup processor will be big enough for all your favorite recipes (including the recipes in this book).

Slow cooker

This will help you create meals when you don't have much time for cooking.

Spiral slicer or julienne vegetable peeler

Using a spiral slicer, foods can easily be made into noodles, which is fun for kids and makes eating vegetables more enjoyable. The most popular brand is the Spiralizer. A julienne peeler can also be used for cutting vegetables into "noodles."

Immersion blender and/or high-speed blender

An immersion blender is a great tool to have. It makes pureeing soups and emulsifying mayo a breeze. And they are available at very affordable prices.

Blendtec and Vitamix are the top options for high-speed blenders, but there are more affordable alternatives. The Nutribullet is compact and affordable, and it does a great job blending frozen fruit and veggies, nuts, and ice.

AND IT'S PERFECT IF YOU DON'T HAVE MUCH COUNTER SPACE

Instant-read thermometer

Cooking steaks and burgers to the perfect temperature doesn't have to be a game of chance. Invest in a good thermometer and you can cook them to the exact temperature every time.

Zester

We use the classic Microplane zester/grater, which removes the zest and grates it at the same time. You can use it for grating citrus zest and fresh ginger root.

Handheld electric mixer or stand mixer

These make whipping up batter and cookie dough a breeze, so your forearm doesn't go numb. The difference between them (besides cost) is that a stand mixer is more flexible. With its attachments for whisking and beating, it allows you to create a multitude of recipes using one tool. You can make brownie mixes and cookies, or use it to make coconut milk whipped cream without burning your arm out.

Another bonus: Because a stand mixer runs on its own with a click of a button, you can do other things while the mixer does its job.

Everything else

These tools are either more commonplace, so they're probably already in your kitchen—we have a feeling you have a few pots and pans kicking around—or more specialized, like an ice cream maker. An ice cream maker is really fun to use, but it's definitely low on the list of necessary Paleo kitchen tools.

Pots and pans

In addition to having a couple of well-seasoned cast-iron skillets, we recommend you have a couple of saucepans and sauté pans in different sizes. And you can never go wrong with a stockpot for large batches of chili or soups.

We use small (8-quart/7.5-l) and medium (12-quart/11.3-l) stockpots.

Mixing bowls

Get a number of them in a wide variety of sizes. Even if you clean as you go, several mixing bowls will come in handy. It's better to have them on hand than find out you don't have enough when you're trying to whip up several recipes in one afternoon.

Rimmed baking sheets and cookie sheets

You can get some great nonstick ones or, for the same easy cleanup, you can line a metal baking sheet with parchment paper. Rimmed baking sheets are also called sheet pans.

We use a half sheet pan. Though sizes vary slightly, they are about 13" by 18 inches (33 by 46 cm).

Ice cream scoop and/or cookie scoop

An ice cream scoop, the mechanical type with a spring-loaded wire scraper, is great not only for scooping homemade ice cream but also for scooping even portions of cookie dough onto parchment paper–lined baking sheets or for making perfect-sized meatballs.

Parchment paper

Cleanup is a breeze with parchment paper.

Nut milk strainer or cheesecloth

(AKA NUT MILK BAG)

Great for creating nut milk.

Mandoline

This tool is great for precision cutting and slicing wafer-thin pieces of food.

Fine-mesh strainer

Useful for straining all sorts of things—from watermelon puree to bone broth.

Bakeware

Standard cupcake tins, brownie pans, Pyrex baking dishes. You need all of these awesome bakeware items so you can enjoy the delectable treats in this book. Because we're prone to experimenting with fun gadgets for the kitchen, we do use a specialized baking tool for one recipe: a checkerboard cake pan with a batter dividing ring for making checkerboard cakes.

Even this is optional, however. If you don't want to invest in a checkerboard cake pan, you can simply make the cake as a solid vanilla or chocolate cake.

Measuring cups (liquid and dry) and measuring spoons

Paleo baking and cooking isn't necessarily a science, but it definitely helps to measure.

Vegetable peeler

In addition to a regular vegetable peeler, we also find a julienne peeler useful for cutting vegetables into "noodles."

Lemon/lime juicer

This is a life-changing tool, and once you use it you will be shocked at how much juice actually comes out of a lemon or lime.

Wooden spoons and rubber spatulas

Wooden spoons are indispensable tools to have in the kitchen because they won't melt while touching your hot pan or release toxic chemicals, as plastic can, and they also won't scratch any of your cookware. Rubber spatulas help you scrape bowls clean, ensuring you get to enjoy every last drop of your brownie batter.

Dutch oven

Chilis, stews, soups, roasts—you name it, you can cook it in a Dutch oven.

Ice cream maker

Even though we've made it possible to make all of our ice creams without a machine, this tool makes it much easier and hassle-free.

We use a Cuisinart.

Coffeepot

This is just so you have adequate energy to cook as many recipes as possible in a day, freeze them, and then have premade homemade Paleo meals ready in a flash.

Leave-in thermometer

Sometimes an instant-read thermometer doesn't help if you are leaving a roast or chicken in the oven for an extended period. Using a leave-in thermometer will ensure that you never overcook your meats.

Ramekins

We use 3½-ounce (90-ml) ramekins for baking desserts. They're also great for organizing your mise en place. You can keep salt in one, chopped herbs in another, and diced vegetables in a third.

Vegetable steamer basket

Steaming vegetables is one of the quickest and simplest ways to cook them, so a steamer basket is a great thing to have around. We didn't include any recipes for steaming veggies because it's so simple, but we rely on it for quick meals.

Tongs

Tongs are an invaluable all-purpose tool in the kitchen. Whether you are flipping chicken or bacon, removing bones from broth, or flipping food on the grill, a pair of tongs is what you'll reach for.

Food scale

A food scale will come to your rescue in the baking department time and time again. Baking is like science. You have to be accurate; otherwise, your delicious cake will turn into a science experiment gone horribly wrong.

George &
Juli's Shopping &
Cooking Tips

Now that you have a shopping list for your
Paleo kitchen makeover, it's time to go find
the best meats and produce possible. But before
you head out, we want to share some shopping
tips with you that we find helpful.

How to Shop Smarter

Most of these tips are just plain ol' good shopping tips, whether you shop at farmers markets, food co-ops, or supermarkets. Some tips, however, like the first one, are meant to help you navigate stores that carry fake foods. Remember, the more you shop at farmers markets, the less you'll be faced with packaged foods. It's easier to be strong when you aren't surrounded by temptations!

Stick to the perimeter of the store.

You will find fresh produce, meat, and seafood along the perimeter of a grocery store. If you begin to wander towards the center, you will come across the prepackaged foods, snack items, and junk food.

Purchase frozen and fresh items.

If there is a produce item you love but do not eat often, we recommend purchasing it frozen. We love buying frozen blueberries to add to smoothies once in a while and frozen Brussels sprouts to thaw and roast for a breakfast of eggs and bacon.

Be adventurous.

Don't be afraid to try something new. As a Paleo eater, you are going to be purchasing a huge amount of vegetables and fruit compared to what you are used to. Let's face it, this can get boring pretty easily if you stick to what you know.

NEVER TRIED KALE BEFORE? Grab a bunch and try sautéing it in a pan with some olive oil and herbs, or bake it in the oven at a low temperature to create kale chips.

Explore the bulk section at your grocery store, food co-op, or natural food store. Bulk sections have items ranging from raw nuts and seeds to dried fruit to flour alternatives. If you are trying out one of these for the first time, grab a bag and fill it up with one serving or enough for a few tastes. There is no need to purchase a ton of an item you have never tried before. You will save money and waste less food if you purchase from the bulk section.

An item that you eat a *lot* of is usually cheaper to purchase in bulk as well.

For example, George goes through raw almonds like crazy. He ends up saving over $1.00 per pound when he purchases them from the bulk section.

Ask questions.

Don't be afraid to ask questions of the folks at your local grocery store or the experts at your farmers market. If you want to know where something came from and it is unclear, ask. If a store employee is unsure or unable to tell you, we recommend not purchasing that item. We are leery of eating food whose origins we don't know. We can almost guarantee that the farmers at your farmers market will be able to answer all of your questions, giving you confidence in the food you purchase.

Make friends with the employees at your grocery store; they will come to know you and share all sorts of fun tips with you. They will be excited to tell you about new produce or a new farm they are sourcing from.

Make a few trips to the grocery store each week.

Purchase what you will be able to eat in the next few days. Nothing is more discouraging than buying fresh, healthy food and then throwing half of it into the trash because you bought more than you could consume or had time to cook.

Once you find your go-to stores and have developed relationships with the staff at those stores, we recommend you stick to them—that way you'll always know you're safe with the food you're purchasing.

Make a list of what you need.
And stick to it! If you are going to be preparing several recipes throughout the week, create a list of all the ingredients you will need. It's easier to plan a few recipes in advance to reduce store trips. That way, you know you can confidently purchase what you'll need for the next several days and won't need to return. Stick to the list, and don't wander anywhere you don't need to be to find those ingredients during your time at the store.

Also, create a list of items you can eat between meals as snacks. This can include raw vegetables and fruits, dried unsweetened and unsulfured fruit, and raw nuts.

dates
almond
butter
bananas

Shopping list
- grass feed beef
- chicken thighs
- spinach
- rosemary
- garlic
- ~~X~~ Thyme

Shopping list
- coconut flour
- eggs
- bacon
- asparagus
- onions
- peppers
- shrimp

SHOPPING TIPS FOR MEAT AND SEAFOOD

Purchase wild-caught fish and seafood and responsibly raised, grass-fed meat. Grass-fed meat is easier to digest and better for your stomach than other meat.

MOST ANIMALS ARE FED CORN, SOY, AND OTHER GRAINS.

Corn syrup and nitrates are found in most hot dogs. We recommend buying nitrate-free and sugar-free hot dogs, such as Applegate brand, if you are going to be eating them and incorporating them into your new lifestyle.

Try to purchase your eggs from a local farmers market, or buy organic, cage-free, omega-3 enriched eggs from your local grocery store.

Don't be afraid of buying canned fish and tuna. Whipping up some Paleo mayonnaise with avocado oil and egg yolks to add to some canned tuna is an easy afternoon meal or snack.

This is a great alternative to buying fresh fish.

DON'T BE AFRAID OF THE EGG YOLK. It contains more than half of the protein found in an egg, and it has plenty of healthy fats, nutrients, and omega-3s to support a healthy body and mind.

Buy locally grown produce.

For the freshest produce, meats, and eggs, your best bet is to head to your local farmers market. Almost every city has a farmers market. Google your zip code and the words "farmers market." Most farmers markets are held at least once a week, if not twice. When you shop at a farmers market, you know you are purchasing food that is currently in season, has not been tampered with, does not contain additives or preservatives, and has been grown in a sustainable way without pesticides or chemicals.

We recommend checking out Local Harvest online as well for a directory of local CSA farms and growers. Some CSAs give you the option of having fresh, local produce delivered to your doorstep or picking it up at a convenient spot, as often as once a week.

Amazon is our number-one resource for everything from kitchen tools and gadgets to bulk grocery items. They have wonderful customer service, and their order tracking is always precise.

Buy online if you can't find items locally.

FOR MEAT

If it is difficult for you to access ethically and responsibly raised meat, we recommend ordering online from TX Bar Organics, US Wellness Meats, or another purveyor of quality meats. They will deliver organic and grass-fed meat directly to your doorstep.

FOR NUTS

Nuts.com has a wide range of raw and roasted nuts, nut and gluten-free flours, coffee and tea, and baking products. Their prices (for nuts in particular) are unbeatable.

FOR COCONUT PRODUCTS

Tropical Traditions is our number-one choice for all coconut products: coconut oil, flour, flakes, butter, and more. They also offer many other grocery items, household items, and skin care products. What we love most about this site are their specials. They usually ship us a free quart of coconut oil with every purchase. Their customer service is unbeatable as well.

FOR PALEO SNACKS, GOODIES, AND TREATS

Steve's Paleo Goods, Paleo Treats, and Eating Evolved are all websites that make eating Paleo while traveling easier and more enjoyable. They also have treats such as chocolates and baked goods that will keep you satisfied while on the Paleo path.

FOR PREPARED PALEO MEALS (AND BACON!)

Check out the Pete's Paleo website. They deliver nationwide and offer local pick-up in San Diego, California.

SHOPPING TIPS FOR FRUITS AND VEGGIES

You can use the following Dirty Dozen Plus and Clean 15 lists to help you be a smarter shopper. These lists, published by the Environmental Working Group, are geared towards produce bought at supermarkets. If you shop at farmers markets, you can ask the farmers about their growing practices. Even if what they sell isn't certified organic, many of them farm very sustainably. If you're confident that your farmer uses as few pesticides as possible, many of the foods on the Dirty Dozen become good choices, even if they aren't certified organic.

Please note, however, that since these lists were not created with Paleo eaters in mind, you will find potatoes on the Dirty Dozen Plus list and corn on the Clean 15 list—both generally considered no-no's for a Paleo diet.

THESE LISTS ARE UPDATED YEARLY. TO CHECK OUT THE LATEST VERSIONS, VISIT WWW.EWG.ORG.

DIRTY DOZEN PLUS

The fruits and vegetables that rank the highest in pesticide load are known as the Dirty Dozen. If you can't afford to buy all organic produce, you should at least buy organic versions of these fourteen items.

1. Apples
2. Strawberries
3. Grapes
4. Celery
5. Peaches
6. Spinach
7. Bell peppers
8. Nectarines
9. Cucumbers
10. Potatoes
11. Cherry tomatoes
12. Hot peppers
13. Kale/collard greens
14. Summer squash

CLEAN 15

This produce has the least amount of pesticide load. If you can't afford to buy organic but you want to be exposed as little as possible to pesticides, these fruits and vegetables—with the exception of corn—should make up a good amount of what you eat. (We kept corn here to preserve the integrity of the list, but we do not recommend it as a normal Paleo food.)

1. Mushrooms
2. Sweet potatoes
3. Cantaloupe
4. Grapefruit
5. Kiwi
6. Eggplant
7. Asparagus
8. Mangoes
9. Papayas
10. Sweet peas, frozen
11. Cabbage
12. Avocados
13. Pineapple
14. Onions
15. Corn

How to Cook Smarter

These useful cooking tips will help you make the most of the wonderful foods you've just brought home. With these tips, we hope to ensure that none of the food you've bought sits in a drawer in your fridge. Your goal should be to use everything you buy before you return to the store. In the process, you will save money and discover new dishes and flavors you love.

Save and repurpose your leftovers and scraps.

You can incorporate nut pulp into many of your baking recipes or some dishes, like green beans, for added texture, taste, and nutrition.

Chop fresh herbs in a food processor and add olive oil or melted and cooled coconut oil, pulsing just to evenly coat the herbs in the oil. Freeze the mixture in an ice cube tray to create easy-to-use portions for use in a future recipe.

Freeze overripe fruit to incorporate into a smoothie or a fruit tart or pie.

Extend the life of your produce.

Store dry, unwashed summer squash and zucchini in a plastic bag and remove as much air as possible by wrapping the bag around the squash. Keep the squash in a crisper drawer for up to 5 days.

When you bring lettuce home, it's best to separate the leaves and wash them in a sink full of cold water. Dry the leaves and then roll them in a clean kitchen towel or paper towels and place in a sealable bag. Keep in an area of the refrigerator where they won't get damaged (tender lettuce is easily crushed by heavier foods and will freeze if kept in a too-cold area of the fridge) and store for up to 1 week.

Asparagus is best stored in water. Without washing the asparagus, cut an inch off of the bottom of the stems and place in a container with 2 inches of water. Cover with a plastic bag and store in the refrigerator for up to 5 days.

Cucumbers need to be wrapped, dry and unwashed, in a paper towel and stored in a plastic bag. Store for up to 1 week in the crisper drawer.

Peppers need to be stored, dry and unwashed, in a plastic bag with perforations. You can store them in the crisper for up to 5 days.

Green onions need to be placed, unwashed, in a container with a couple inches of water. Cover and store in the refrigerator for up to 1 week.

Buy quality kitchen equipment and tools.

If your kitchen tools and equipment don't work well and are frustrating to use, you won't enjoy cooking, or at least not as much. Quality doesn't necessarily mean expensive. Do some research and price comparison, and then take the plunge to invest in the good stuff—at least for those things that you turn to daily.

To get an idea of what you will use a lot to make the recipes in this book, check out our top ten tools and equipment on page 38.

Clean as you go.

Nothing is more discouraging than spending hours cleaning up the giant mess you just made in your kitchen.

WE RECOMMEND CLEANING AS YOU GO TO SAVE YOUR SANITY AT THE END: RINSE DISHES, LOAD UP THE DISHWASHER, AND PUT AWAY ITEMS YOU ARE NO LONGER USING.

Mix it up.

Try cooking all that new food and those new recipes in different ways. You can cook something as simple as eggs in so many different ways: scrambled, fried, over easy, soft- or hard-boiled, poached, and so on. Experiment with that chicken breast you have been grilling over and over again or those veggies you keep steaming. Bust out the slow cooker, turn on your stove, and get out the skillet with a slick of duck fat. You won't get bored if you don't let yourself. Don't be intimidated by the items in your kitchen—you are bigger than they are.

Purchase plenty of storage containers.

If you cannot efficiently store all this new and delicious food, what's the point of making it? Tupperware is going to be your new best friend.

Mason jars and airtight containers are great for storing nuts, spices, and even some of the Paleo flours.

Keep your refrigerator, freezer, and pantry organized.

Keep the vegetables with the fruit and all the meat together in a cool drawer. It will be much easier for you to prepare recipes and rummage through your refrigerator and freezer if you know that like items are kept together.

Freeze your items as flat as possible. Keep them in flat, airtight containers, and you will be able to stack them more neatly.

Get yourself a label maker or chalkboard labels so you can label and date all your bulk food containers. That way, you'll never mix up your almond flour and coconut flour.

REFRIGERATOR

Apples	Cauliflower	Grapes
Beans	Celery	Jalapeños
Berries	Cherries	Leafy greens
Broccoli	Cucumbers	Mushrooms
Cabbage	Eggplants	Zucchini
Carrots	Ginger	

ROOM TEMPERATURE OR COOL PANTRY

Apricots	Plums
Avocados	Sweet potatoes
Bananas	Winter squash
Citrus	
Garlic	
Kiwi	
Melons	
Nectarines	
Onions	
Peaches	
Pears	
Pineapples	

We like to treat our meat like royalty. The protein is the most expensive part of the meal and should be treated accordingly so there is no waste. Part of this lifestyle is respecting our food, and there is no better way than by using it all.

Get to know different cuts and parts of the meat and the flavors each of them will bring to the table. For example, chicken thighs and chicken breasts have dissimilar tastes, and you can create different delicious recipes for these parts of the chicken.

Partially freeze meat before you cut into it. Throwing meat into the freezer for 15 to 30 minutes before you plan on cutting into it should do the trick.

This makes the meat much easier to cut.

Whip up some delicious bone broth using those animal bones.

If you are cooking meat and it is coming out a little tough, add a bit of vinegar to help tenderize it. Ten minutes before you begin cooking any meat, add 1 tablespoon of vinegar for each quarter-pound of meat. You can also experiment with flavors by using balsamic vinegar, wine vinegar, or apple cider vinegar. All will be delicious and give you variety in your cooking.

If you are not going to eat the meat, poultry, fish, or seafood you have purchased before the sell-by date, throw it in the freezer. You can freeze it for up to a year, and it will taste as good as newly bought after you thaw it out again.

WE LIKE TO PLACE A STICKY NOTE ON THE ITEM AND WRITE THE DATE WITH A BLACK PERMANENT MARKER, SO WE CAN'T MISS IT.

Read through the recipe you are using several times before you begin.

Make sure you read through each step and check that you have each of the ingredients the recipe calls for. You don't want to have to run to the store in the middle of cooking something or risk not being able to complete the recipe.

Also make sure that you have the correct tools to execute the recipe. If the recipe calls for a high-speed blender like a Vitamix, determine if you can improvise with an immersion blender or something like a Magic Bullet.

Take care of your knives, and use the appropriate cutting surface.

The sharper your knife is, the harder it will be for you to cut yourself. If you're using your knives every day, they should be sharpened once a week and honed with a steel before every use. If you use your knives just a few days a week, then sharpening them every other week is fine, but honing has to occur every time you use them. ←

YouTube videos are a great source for learning how to sharpen and hone blades—that's where I learned.

Level off dry ingredients when measuring them.

In this book, teaspoon, tablespoon, and cup quantities of dry ingredients, such as flours, are measured by using the spoon or cup measure to scoop up the ingredient and leveling the top with the back of a knife or your finger.

Taste your food as you go.

Why wait until the finished product is ready to taste your creation? Taste your food as you go to ensure you are creating something you will love.

1. CONSISTENCY

2. MODERATION

Sticking to Paleo

In the four years that we have been on our
Paleo journeys, we have learned a lot about
the challenges of staying on a Paleo diet.
Throughout this book we will share lots of tips
with you about how to stay on track, but if we
had to narrow it down to the top four things
that have helped us tremendously in sticking
with Paleo, it would be these:

3. BALANCE

4. EXERCISE

1. CONSISTENCY

The more often you eat Paleo and the more often you cook Paleo meals, the easier it will become to stick with Paleo. Once you become familiar with Paleo ingredient choices—those to eat daily and those to avoid—you'll find it easier to make choices at restaurants because you'll know how to turn the restaurant's offerings into your own Paleo meal. Before you know it, eating Paleo will become second nature.

2. MODERATION

Remember that just because you are eating something that is Paleo, it doesn't mean that you can eat three times as much. That goes for the cookies, the pancakes, and even the savory foods, like chili. Just as with any healthy diet that has ever been marketed, moderation is key to finding a healthy balance within your body.

IN "EATING OUT PALEO STYLE" ON PAGE 66, WE'VE INCLUDED LOTS OF TIPS FOR DINING OUT AND KEEPING TO A PALEO DIET.

3. BALANCE

Just because you have taken on this new lifestyle choice doesn't mean that your friends have, or even that they want to hear about it. So when you head to a potluck or a friend's house and they bring out their famous homemade pizza and chocolate cupcakes, there is no need to be rude. If you are being strict with your diet, explain to them that you won't be able to have any this time around. Or maybe, since it's only once a year that they make this food, have a couple bites (as long as you know it won't bug your stomach too much).

4. EXERCISE

Both of us are huge advocates of exercise. We fully believe everyone should move every day. Whether it's a walk around your neighborhood, weightlifting, spin class, CrossFit, kickboxing, or really anything that keeps your muscles strong, we want you to do it.

Dash

community.

Cooking with Others

We believe cooking with another person makes cooking more fun, and fun is what will help you stick with your new Paleo lifestyle. Here are some reasons to cook with another person and ways to have fun the entire time you're in the kitchen.

You have someone to dance with in the kitchen.

In our duo, Juli does most of the dancing George just changes the music.

Someone can clean while the other person cooks. That means less time spent cleaning at the end of the meal.

George likes to sneak in and clean up behind Juli, interrupting her cooking Zen.

Cooking parties or cooking with friends makes cooking more fun. You get the pleasure of sharing what you've just made and the excitement of getting immediate feedback.

OUR FAVORITE SHARING PARTY WAS WHEN WE MADE MULTIPLE DESSERTS EVERY DAY AND THEN ATE THEM.

Two heads are better than one when it comes to flavor creations.

You can delegate tasks. When someone is chopping the vegetables, another person can be setting the table.

More food is possible with two pairs of helping hands. *AND WHO DOESN'T LOVE MORE FOOD?*

When you cook alongside someone—husband, wife, friend, family member, boyfriend, new friend, old friend, son, daughter, whoever— you create lasting memories and positive associations with cooking.

If you burn something or a recipe fails, you have a friend to laugh with. And someone to go grab a bite with.

Eating Out Paleo Style

Who wants to be a pizza party pooper or a margarita night mope? Not us. It can be a rarity that we get to spend the night out with close friends. Sometimes you may get to choose the restaurant you all go to, but other times, you need to be a little more lenient in order to keep your friends happy. No need to spoil the evening because of your own personal dietary restrictions and choices.

Even though we've pressed the point of staying consistent during your Paleo journey, we've also talked about balance. And balancing your friendships and relationships while still pursuing your goals is incredibly important when it comes to sticking with Paleo. If you are still able to go out with friends and enjoy your nights out, you are more likely to stick with your dietary habits outside of restaurants and bars.

We all find ourselves at restaurants for different reasons. Some may end up at a nearby sushi restaurant three to five times a week to discuss business plans with clients. Some may be enjoying a Sunday brunch with family. And some people may just be completely sick of cooking for the week and head out to a local Mexican joint. We all have different reasons for going out, but finding the right food at a restaurant will give us the confidence to keep spending time with friends at restaurants. If you are eating out on a regular basis, make sure to stay consistent with your Paleo guidelines as much as possible. If you are going out once a month, maybe splurge a little. Life is all about living.

We want you to enjoy yourself when you're eating out Paleo style, so we've come up with several useful tips as well as guidance for ordering food at specific types of restaurants. Scrambling to come up with something to order off a menu, when a server is standing there waiting for you to make a decision, is not fun. Why not take the pressure off? If you know you are going to be eating out quite often, have some order ideas in mind. This makes the whole process more enjoyable. Most restaurants post their menus online, making it easy to preview a menu and come up with ideas in advance.

The bottom line is that you are in charge of the way you make your body feel. Why not ensure a happy mind and healthy belly by ordering your food accordingly?

BUT DON'T FORGET ABOUT BALANCE. SPLURGING A LITTLE BIT ON SPECIAL OCCASIONS IS OKAY.

HERE ARE SOME TIPS TO HELP YOU STICK WITH PALEO DURING YOUR FUN NIGHTS OUT:

Be sure to have some kind of protein and a veggie on your plate.

Try to drink as much water as possible during your meal.
It may sound crazy, but having more water in your stomach will help you feel full faster *and* keep you away from the chips or other appetizers that may be sitting on the table.

Always have a backup plan.
If you get to the restaurant and find out there is absolutely nothing there for you to eat, be sure to have something that you can snack on in your purse, your backpack, or even your car.

This will keep you from going off the deep end.

If you are involved in the planning process, try to pick a restaurant that uses fresh ingredients.
You can search on "artisan" or "farm to table" to find a place that uses fresh and local ingredients.

Try not to show up hungry.
The hungrier you are, the more likely you are to make a bad food choice because you aren't thinking clearly.

Bring some fruit or eat a snack before you leave so you're not tempted while others are eating the restaurant's bread.

Don't assume that because you've ordered meat or veggies, your meal is gluten-free or Paleo.
Restaurants often dust their foods with flour before cooking, so be safe and ask questions.

If you are going to drink alcohol, go with an option that won't distress your stomach the next day or cause you to deviate from your Paleo lifestyle.
In keeping with Paleo, avoid beer (unless gluten-free), alcohols that are distilled from grain or sugar (such as whiskeys, bourbon, or rum), and mixers made with sugar or corn syrup. Many cocktails are made with simple syrup, so always ask if there's sugar in a cocktail. Our personal go-to choices are organic wine, tequila with club soda and lime, or non-grain-distilled vodkas mixed with club soda. Two good vodka options are Cîroc, which is distilled from grapes, and VuQo, which is distilled from coconut. Keep in mind that alcohol means sugar, so just as with any other treat, you must use moderation when consuming alcohol.

THIS WILL HELP YOU WITH YOUR GOAL, WHETHER IT'S WEIGHT LOSS OR JUST LIVING A HEALTHIER, PALEO LIFESTYLE.

Skip the Chips!

Here are some helpful hints about what to avoid on restaurant menus and ideas for what to order when eating out.

BREAKFAST/BRUNCH

Eggs ← fried, scrambled, hard-boiled, poached

Bacon

Ham

Steak

Sausage ← *MAKE SURE IT IS GLUTEN-FREE*

Fruit or sliced tomatoes as a side

Omelets or frittatas ← *ask if the omelets are just eggs; a lot of restaurants add flour or pancake batter as a secret ingredient to make eggs fluffy*

LUNCH/DINNER

Thai ← *MAKE SURE SAUCES ARE MADE FROM SCRATCH*

Avoid rice and tofu.

Look for a coconut-based curry dish (hold the rice) with beef, chicken, pork, or seafood. Add more veggies to fill the void of rice.

Soups and salads

Indian ← *MAKE SURE SAUCES ARE MADE FROM SCRATCH*

Chicken tikka masala

Tandoori chicken ← *OR SHRIMP*

Chicken, lamb, or vegetable curry

Japanese

Rolls wrapped in cucumber or seaweed—just ask for the rolls to be made without rice

Sashimi

Meat and veggie skewers, which are often an appetizer option

Italian

Grilled or baked chicken, fish, or steak

Order spaghetti with meatballs, hold the pasta and replace with vegetables. ← *just ask if there are breadcrumbs in the meatballs*

Ciopinno

Mexican

Steer clear of the chips and salsa. Not only is it a tough appetizer to put down, but the chips are often fried in vegetable oils.

Chicken, steak, or shrimp fajitas with no rice and beans ↖

Hold the rice and beans and add guacamole and pico de gallo.

Burrito without the tortilla, rice, and beans. Many places will gladly put it in a bowl instead.

Steak or taco salad without the taco shell

Order a taco with the best ingredients, and just don't eat the shell.

Chinese

This is the hardest kind of restaurant to find Paleo options at. Some Chinese restaurants offer some gluten-free options to choose from.

NOT THE BEST OPTION, BUT BETTER THAN MOST.

If worse comes to worst, you can always bring coconut aminos with you and add it to plain steamed veggies and meat.

American

Burger with no bun, lots of toppings, and sub veggies for French fries. If you can find a restaurant that cooks sweet potato fries in a good fat such as lard or duck fat, or even just bakes them, feel free to choose those. Restaurants often use vegetable fat for frying.

Steer clear of ketchup. ↖ *IT'S LIKELY TO HAVE CORN SYRUP OR SUGAR IN IT*

Sandwiches wrapped in lettuce or on greens

Steak and vegetables

Seafood or fish and vegetables

Salad without dressing or with vinegar and olive oil, if possible

BBQ

Stick with meats that are grilled or smoked and aren't covered in sauces.

YOU CAN MAKE AN EXCEPTION IF THEY MAKE THEIR SAUCES IN-HOUSE AND YOU ARE OKAY WITH THE INGREDIENTS.

Breakfast

Sun-Dried Tomato
Sweet Potato Hash

serves: **4** | prep time: **20 minutes** | cook time: **20 minutes**

Ingredients

4 ounces (115 grams) pancetta, finely chopped

1 large sweet potato, cut into ½-inch (12-mm) dice

½ yellow onion, diced

4 ounces (115 grams) sun-dried tomatoes (in oil and drained)

coarse sea salt and freshly ground black pepper, to taste

4 large eggs (optional)

¼ cup (about 10 grams) fresh basil leaves, roughly chopped, for garnish

Process

1. Brown the pancetta in a cast-iron skillet over medium-high heat, then add the diced sweet potato. Stir the sweet potatoes to coat them in the rendered fat.

2. Cover the pan with a lid and cook for 5 minutes, then remove the lid and continue to cook, flipping the sweet potatoes with a wooden spoon until the sweet potatoes are brown on all sides, about 10 minutes.

3. Once the sweet potatoes are browned, add the onion and sun-dried tomatoes. Sprinkle with salt and pepper and mix well.

4. Cook for another 5 minutes or until the onions have softened and become translucent. If you choose to add eggs to this hash, create 4 wells in the hash, then carefully crack the eggs into the wells, cover with a lid, and cook until the eggs are cooked to preference. Before serving, garnish with the chopped basil.

Banana Bread Waffles with Mixed Fruit Topping

makes: **8 (4½-inch/11-cm) Belgian waffles or 16 (4½-inch/11-cm) standard waffles** | prep time: **5 minutes** | cook time: **15 minutes**

Ingredients

4 large bananas, mashed

4 large eggs

½ cup (140 grams) almond butter

¼ cup (50 grams) melted coconut oil, plus more for greasing the waffle iron

½ cup (75 grams) coconut flour

1 tablespoon ground cinnamon

1 teaspoon baking soda

1 teaspoon baking powder

1 teaspoon vanilla extract

pinch of fine-grain sea salt

For the toppings

1 cup (170 grams) blueberries, plus extra for garnish (optional)

1½ cups (340 grams) raspberries, plus extra for garnish (optional)

2 teaspoons coconut oil

2 tablespoons organic honey

2 tablespoons coconut oil

1 banana, sliced

1 teaspoon ground cinnamon

Process

1. Preheat the waffle iron.

2. Combine the bananas, eggs, almond butter, and coconut oil in a blender, food processor, or mixing bowl and mix well until smooth. Add the coconut flour, cinnamon, baking soda, baking powder, vanilla, and salt and mix until the batter is smooth.

3. Lightly brush the waffle iron with melted coconut oil. Using the manufacturer's guidelines for suggested cup (or milliliter) quantity, ladle the batter into the preheated and greased waffle iron, and spread it evenly across the surface, leaving a ½-inch (12-mm) border (the batter will spread when you close the lid). Cook, following the manufacturer's directions, and set aside on a plate and keep warm while you cook the remaining waffles.

4. While the waffles are cooking, make the toppings: Place the blueberries and raspberries in a blender or food processor and blend until the berries break down completely and the mixture is smooth. Place the pureed berries and honey in a small saucepan. Mix together and cook over medium heat until the berry mixture begins to bubble, stirring often, then turn the heat down to low and let it thicken, about 10 minutes.

5. Heat the coconut oil in a small saucepan over medium heat. Once the oil is hot, add the banana slices and sprinkle with the cinnamon. Cook on both sides for less than a minute, just until the bananas caramelize.

6. Serve the waffles with the mixed berry and banana toppings, and garnish with extra berries, if desired.

Pumpkin Waffles

makes: **5 (4½-inch/11-cm) Belgian waffles or 10 (4½-inch/11-cm) standard waffles** | prep time: **5 minutes** | cook time: **15 minutes**

Ingredients

2 large bananas, mashed

½ cup (120 ml) pumpkin puree

5 large eggs

½ cup (125 grams) almond butter

¼ cup (50 grams) melted coconut oil, plus more for greasing the waffle iron

½ cup (75 grams) coconut flour

2 tablespoons pumpkin pie spice

1 teaspoon baking soda

1 teaspoon baking powder

1 teaspoon vanilla extract

pinch of fine-grain sea salt

maple syrup, for serving

Process

1. Preheat the waffle iron.

2. Combine the bananas, pumpkin puree, eggs, almond butter, and coconut oil in a food processor or blender and process until the bananas are well blended with the other ingredients. Once smooth, add the coconut flour, pumpkin pie spice, baking soda, baking powder, vanilla, and salt and blend until well mixed.

3. Lightly brush the waffle iron with melted coconut oil. Using the manufacturer's guidelines for suggested cup (or milliliter) quantity, ladle the batter into the preheated and greased waffle iron and spread it evenly across the surface, leaving a ½-inch (12-mm) border (the batter will spread when you close the lid). Cook, following the manufacturer's directions, and set aside on a plate and keep warm while you cook the remaining waffles.

Baked Banana Chip
Crusted French Toast

makes: **6 to 8 slices** | prep time: **35+ minutes** | cook time: **15 to 18 minutes**

Ingredients

1 cup (65 grams) banana chips

1 large egg

2 tablespoons full-fat coconut milk

1 teaspoon vanilla extract

⅛ teaspoon ground cinnamon

pinch of fine-grain sea salt

6 to 8 (¾-inch/2-cm thick) slices leftover banana bread (see Note)

Process

1. Preheat the oven to 350°F (175°C). Line a rimmed baking sheet with parchment paper.

2. Place the banana chips in a food processor and pulse until you have banana chip bits (you should not have a powder). Place the crushed chips in a shallow bowl or plate.

3. Whisk together the egg, coconut milk, vanilla, cinnamon, and salt in another shallow bowl.

4. Dip a slice of banana bread into the egg mixture, coat on both sides, then do the same in the crushed banana chips, making sure the slice is completely covered with banana chips. Place on the prepared baking sheet and repeat with the rest of the slices.

5. Bake for 15 to 18 minutes or until the banana chips have slightly browned. Serve with maple syrup or eat as-is.

note:

Any leftover Paleo banana bread will do. You can use our recipe for Cinnamon Chocolate Swirl Banana Bread on page 81; just omit the cinnamon chocolate swirl ingredients.

Cinnamon Chocolate Swirl
Banana Bread

makes: **1 (9-by-5-inch/23-by-12-cm) loaf** | prep time: **10 minutes** | cook time: **45 minutes**

Ingredients

coconut oil, to grease the pan

For the banana bread

4 medium bananas (about 1 pound/455 grams)

4 large eggs

¼ cup (½ stick/50 grams) unsalted grass-fed butter, melted

½ cup (125 grams) almond butter

⅓ cup (60 grams) coconut flour

1 teaspoon baking soda

1 teaspoon baking powder

1 teaspoon vanilla extract

pinch of fine-grain sea salt

For the swirl

2 tablespoons unsalted grass-fed butter

2 tablespoons ground cinnamon

½ cup (3½ ounces/100 grams) Enjoy Life Mini Chocolate Chips

1 tablespoon organic honey

Process

1. Preheat the oven to 350°F (175°C). Grease a 9-by-5-inch (23-by-12-cm) metal loaf pan and line it with parchment paper.

2. Combine the bananas, eggs, butter, and almond butter in a food processor or mixing bowl and mix until the ingredients are well blended. Add the coconut flour, baking soda, baking powder, vanilla, and salt and continue to mix until all the ingredients are well combined.

3. In a double boiler over medium-low heat, mix together the swirl ingredients. Heat, stirring often, until the chocolate has melted.

4. Pour the bread batter into the prepared pan and spread it out evenly. As soon as you pour the batter, pour the chocolate swirl directly on top and use a knife to swirl the chocolate throughout the loaf pan.

5. Bake for 45 minutes, or until a toothpick comes out clean when inserted in the middle. Remove from the oven and let cool in the pan on a cooling rack for 15 minutes before serving.

Sweet Potato Quiche

serves: **6 to 8** | prep time: **20 minutes** | cook time: **35 to 40 minutes**

Ingredients

3 sweet potatoes (1⅓ lb/600 grams)

About ⅓ cup (75 ml) coconut oil, divided, plus extra for greasing the springform pan

12 ounces (340 grams) Brussels sprouts, cut in half

2 pinches plus 1 teaspoon coarse sea salt

4 to 5 cups (160 to 200 grams) spinach, roughly chopped

1 cup (30 grams) fresh basil leaves, roughly chopped, plus an additional handful of leaves, chopped, for garnish

10 large eggs

1 teaspoon garlic powder

½ teaspoon cayenne pepper

2 teaspoons freshly ground black pepper

Process

1. Preheat the oven to 375°F (190°C).

2. Cut the sweet potatoes lengthwise into wafer-thin planks (a mandoline helps with this task).

3. Heat 2 tablespoons of the coconut oil in a large sauté pan over medium heat. Place 4 to 5 sweet potato slices in the pan and cook for less than a minute on each side, just until the sweet potatoes become soft. Once they are soft, remove to a paper towel–lined plate to drain. Repeat with the rest of the sweet potatoes, adding more coconut oil to the pan as needed.

4. Once all the sweet potatoes slices are cooked, grease a springform pan thoroughly with coconut oil. Line the bottom of the pan with sweet potato slices until completely covered, then line the sides of the pan with sweet potato slices. If you are having trouble getting the sweet potatoes to stick to the side of the pan, use a bit more coconut oil to get them to stay in place.

5. In the same pan the sweet potatoes were cooked in, heat 2 tablespoons of the coconut oil over medium heat and sauté the Brussels sprouts with a pinch of salt until slightly browned, about 10 minutes. Once browned, add the spinach and basil along with another pinch of salt and let cook for less than a minute, just to wilt. Remove from the heat to cool to room temperature.

6. Whisk the eggs in a large bowl along with garlic powder, cayenne pepper, 1 teaspoon of salt, and pepper. Add the vegetable mixture to the eggs and mix well.

7. Set the springform pan on top of a rimmed baking sheet to catch any spills and pour the egg mixture into the pan. Bake for 35 to 40 minutes or until the eggs are firm in the middle. Let rest for 10 to 15 minutes before serving. Garnish with the chopped fresh basil leaves.

Delicata Squash Frittata

serves: **6 to 8** | prep time: **20 minutes** | cook time: **12 minutes**

Ingredients

1 pound (455 grams) ground pork

coarse sea salt and freshly ground black pepper, to taste

1 small delicata squash (about 9 ounces/255 grams), cut into ¼-inch (6-mm) slices (skin can stay on)

6 large eggs

2 tablespoons roughly chopped fresh chives, plus 1 or 2 extra chives for garnish (optional)

Process

1. Preheat the oven to 350°F (175°C).

2. Place a large cast-iron skillet over medium heat. Once the pan is hot, add the ground pork and sprinkle with a pinch of salt. Break up the meat into small pieces with a spatula and cook until no pink remains. Use a slotted spoon to remove the pork from the pan and set aside. Leave 2 tablespoons of fat in the pan for cooking the squash.

3. Using a spoon, scoop out the seeds and excess strings from the squash slices. Reheat the cast-iron skillet with the reserved fat over medium heat and place the delicata rounds throughout the pan, leaving about ½ inch (12 mm) between the slices. Cook the rounds for about 3 to 4 minutes per side. Once squash has slightly browned and is soft, remove the pan from the heat.

4. In a large bowl, whisk together the eggs, chopped chives, and a generous pinch of salt and pepper. Add the ground pork to the egg mixture and whisk to combine.

5. Pour the egg mixture into the cast-iron skillet with the delicata squash rounds. Place in the oven and bake for 10 to 12 minutes, or until the eggs are firm to the touch in the middle. Let rest for a few minutes before slicing into 6 to 8 pie slices. Snip fresh chives over the top for garnish, if desired.

Lavender Vanilla Bean Granola

serves: **4** | prep time: **10 minutes** | cook time: **15 minutes**

Ingredients

1 cup (100 grams) sliced almonds

1 cup (100 grams) chopped walnuts

½ cup (80 grams) pitted dates, chopped

⅓ cup (20 grams) unsweetened shredded coconut

¼ cup (20 grams) blanched almond flour

¼ cup (50 grams) coconut oil, melted

2 tablespoons maple syrup

1 teaspoon vanilla extract

2 tablespoons dried lavender buds (see Notes)

seeds from 1 vanilla bean (see Notes)

pinch of ground cinnamon

pinch of fine-grain sea salt

Process

1. Preheat the oven to 350°F (175°C). Line a rimmed baking sheet with parchment paper.

2. Place all the ingredients in a large bowl and mix well. Turn the mixture out onto the prepared baking sheet and spread it into an even layer. Bake for 15 minutes. Let cool completely before serving to ensure that the granola will harden into clusters.

notes:

lavender is a member of the mint family and is closely related to rosemary, sage, and thyme. Make sure you buy culinary-grade lavender buds, which can be found in bulk at some health food stores or online. They can be used like any spice in baking or cooking, such as in muffins and soups. Just use sparingly, as a little goes a long way.

To remove the seeds from the vanilla bean, use a paring knife to slit the bean down the middle and then, with the tip of the knife, scrape the seeds from the bean.

Lemon Raspberry
Swirl Muffins

makes: **9 muffins** | prep time: **10 minutes** | cook time: **25 to 30 minutes**

Ingredients

½ cup (**55 grams**) coconut flour, sifted

½ cup (**65 grams**) coconut sugar

5 large eggs, whisked

juice of 2 lemons

zest of 1 lemon

1 teaspoon vanilla extract

1 teaspoon baking soda

pinch of fine-grain sea salt

1 cup (125 grams) raspberries

2 tablespoons organic honey

Process

1. Preheat the oven to 350°F (175° C). Line 9 wells of a muffin tin with paper liners.

2. In a large bowl, mix together the coconut flour, coconut sugar, eggs, lemon juice and zest, vanilla, baking soda, and salt until smooth. Pour the batter into the lined wells of the muffin tin.

3. In a blender, puree the raspberries and honey until smooth. Use a spoon to add about a tablespoon of the raspberry puree on top of each muffin, then use a knife to swirl the raspberry through the batter.

4. Bake for 25 to 30 minutes, or until a toothpick comes out nearly clean when inserted in the middle. Let cool in the muffin tin on a cooling rack before removing and serving. Store leftovers in an airtight container for up to 5 days.

Vanilla White
Peach Muffins

makes: **10 muffins** | prep time: **10 minutes** | cook time: **20 to 23 minutes**

Ingredients

½ cup (**1 stick/100 grams**) unsalted grass-fed butter or coconut oil, softened

½ cup (**120 ml**) Grade B maple syrup

2 large eggs

1 teaspoon vanilla extract

1 cup (**120 grams**) tapioca flour

¼ cup (**30 grams**) coconut flour

1 teaspoon baking powder

pinch of fine-grain sea salt

½ cup (**80 grams**) diced dried white peaches

Process

1. Preheat the oven to 350°F (175°C). Line 10 wells of a muffin tin with paper liners.

2. In a large bowl, mix together the softened butter, maple syrup, eggs, and vanilla with an electric mixer or whisk until the mixture is smooth.

3. In a separate bowl, whisk together the tapioca flour, coconut flour, baking powder, and salt. Slowly add the dry mixture to the wet mixture, ¼ cup (30 grams) at a time, until well mixed. Fold in the diced peaches.

4. Using an ice cream scoop, fill the lined wells of the muffin tin. Divide any remaining batter evenly among the lined wells.

5. Bake for 20 to 23 minutes, or until a toothpick comes out clean when inserted in the middle of a muffin. Remove the muffins from the muffin tin and place on a cooling rack until ready to serve. Store leftovers in an airtight container for up to 5 days at room temperature.

Biscuits
& Gravy

serves: **8** | prep time: **45 minutes** | cook time: **25 minutes**

Ingredients

For the biscuits

1 large sweet potato or yam (about 14 ounces/400 grams)

3 large eggs, whisked

3 tablespoons coconut oil, melted

2 tablespoons finely chopped fresh rosemary

1 tablespoon fresh thyme leaves

3 tablespoons coconut flour

1 teaspoon baking powder

pinch of fine-grain sea salt and freshly ground black pepper

For the gravy

8 ounces (225 grams) Italian sausage or your favorite sausage, loose

1 tablespoon coconut flour

1 (14-ounce/415-ml) can full-fat coconut milk

1 teaspoon dried sage

½ teaspoon garlic powder

3 tablespoons arrowroot powder, divided

coarse sea salt and freshly ground black pepper, to taste

Process

1. Preheat the oven to 400°F (205°C).

2. Make the biscuits: Using a fork, poke holes in the sweet potato. Bake for 45 to 50 minutes or until soft. Remove from the oven and reduce the heat to 375°F (190°C).

3. Once the sweet potato is cool enough to handle, remove the skin and add the flesh to a bowl. Mash with a fork until smooth. (You should have 2 cups/400 grams.) Add the eggs and coconut oil to the mashed sweet potatoes and mix well. Then fold in the rosemary and thyme. Lastly, mix in the coconut flour, baking powder, and salt and pepper.

4. Line a baking sheet with parchment paper. Using a large ice cream scoop, scoop out a full scoop of the biscuit mixture and place on the prepared baking sheet. Repeat with the remaining dough, placing the biscuits 1 inch apart. You should have 8 biscuits. Bake for 25 minutes, or until a tester inserted in the center comes out clean.

5. While the biscuits are baking, make the gravy: Brown the sausage in a large sauté pan over medium heat, breaking it up into pieces with a spatula as it cooks. Once the sausage is fully cooked, sprinkle with the coconut flour to soak up some of the excess oil. Mix the flour into the sausage.

6. Add the coconut milk to the sausage and mix well. Then whisk in the sage and garlic powder. To thicken the gravy, add the arrowroot powder, tablespoon by tablespoon, whisking until the coconut milk thickens a bit. Add a pinch of salt and pepper, tasting to make sure it's seasoned to your preference. Serve the gravy over split sweet potato biscuits.

Fluffy Blueberry Pancakes

makes: **5 (3-inch/7-5-cm) pancakes** | prep time: **5 minutes** | cook time; **15 minutes**

Ingredients

3 large eggs

½ cup (120 ml) + 3 tablespoons almond or full-fat coconut milk

1 tablespoon organic honey

½ tablespoon freshly squeezed lemon juice

1 teaspoon vanilla extract

½ cup (60 grams) coconut flour

½ cup (65 grams) tapioca flour

½ teaspoon baking powder

½ teaspoon baking soda

pinch of fine-grain sea salt

coconut oil, for greasing the skillet

½ cup (75 grams) fresh blueberries

Coconut Butter (page 305), for serving

maple syrup, for garnish (optional)

Process

1. In a large bowl, whisk the eggs. Add the almond milk, honey, lemon juice, and vanilla and whisk until well blended. In a separate bowl, mix together the coconut flour and tapioca flour, then add to the wet ingredients ¼ cup (60 grams) at a time, while continuously whisking. Then mix in the baking powder, baking soda, and salt.

2. Grease a large skillet and place over medium heat. Once the skillet is hot, use a ladle to pour 3-inch (7.5-cm) pancakes into the skillet. Once holes begin to appear in the surface of a pancake, drop a small handful of blueberries onto it and flip it. The pancake should cook on each side for 3 to 4 minutes. Repeat with rest of the batter.

3. Top with coconut butter and maple syrup, if desired.

Bacon Sweet Potato Hash with Apples & Pears

serves: **4** | prep time: **30 minutes** | cook time: **10 minutes**

Ingredients

2 sweet potatoes (14 ounces/ 400 grams), cubed

2 tablespoons coconut oil, melted

6 slices thick-cut bacon, cut crosswise into lardons ¼ inch (6 mm) wide

1 Fuji apple, cored and diced

1 pear, cored and diced

1 medium sweet onion, sliced

2 teaspoons ground cinnamon

coarse sea salt, to taste

zest of 1 lemon

juice of ½ lemon

Process

1. Preheat the oven to 400°F (205°C). Line a rimmed baking sheet with parchment paper.

2. In a mixing bowl, toss the cubed sweet potatoes in the coconut oil to coat well.

3. Spread the sweet potatoes out on the prepared baking sheet. Bake for 30 minutes, stirring once at the 15-minute mark, until the sweet potatoes can be easily pierced with a fork.

4. Once the sweet potatoes are done, cook the bacon lardons in a cast-iron skillet over medium heat for 3 to 4 minutes, stirring constantly. Add the apple, pear, and onion and saute for another 2 to 3 minutes, until the onion starts to soften. Add the sweet potatoes, cinnamon, and a pinch of salt and stir well. Cook for 1 to 2 minutes more, stirring occasionally. Taste for seasoning and add more salt if desired.

5. Remove from the heat, add the lemon zest and juice, and mix well before serving.

Cinnamon Rolls

makes: **6 cinnamon rolls** | prep time: **15 to 20 minutes** | cook time: **17 to 20 minutes**

Ingredients

2½ cups (240 grams) blanched almond flour, plus extra for the work surface

¼ cup (30 grams) coconut flour

¼ cup (30 grams) tapioca flour

¼ teaspoon baking soda

pinch of fine-grain sea salt

3 large eggs, at room temperature

¼ cup (50 grams) coconut oil, melted

3 tablespoons organic honey, melted

For the filling

2 tablespoons coconut oil, melted

¼ cup (60 ml) + 1 tablespoon organic honey, melted

2 tablespoons ground cinnamon

½ cup (60 grams) pecans, crushed or minced in a food processor

Coconut Butter (page 305), melted, for serving

Process

1. Preheat the oven to 350°F (175°C). Line a baking sheet with parchment paper.

2. In a large bowl, combine the almond flour, coconut flour, tapioca flour, baking soda, and salt and stir well.

3. In a separate bowl, whisk together the eggs, coconut oil, and honey. Pour the wet ingredients into the large bowl with almond flour mixture. Mix well and then use your hands to knead the dough in the bowl until it is smooth. It may seem sticky, but it will smooth out. Place the dough in the refrigerator for 10 to 15 minutes to make it easier to work with.

4. While the dough is in the refrigerator, make the filling: In a small mixing bowl, combine the coconut oil, honey, cinnamon, and pecans and mix well. Set the bowl in a warm water bath to keep the filling at a pourable consistency while you form and bake the rolls.

5. Place a long piece of parchment paper (about 18 inches/46 cm) on the counter and sprinkle with a little almond flour. Remove the dough from the refrigerator and place on the floured parchment paper. Sprinkle a little almond flour on top of the dough, place another piece of parchment paper on top of it, and gently roll the dough out to an even 10-by-15-inch (25-by-38-cm) rectangle. The dough should be about ¼ inch (6 mm) thick. Take a *lot* of time on this step as the dough is fragile.

6. Trim the edges to make the dough a perfect rectangle and patch any torn spots. Remove the top piece of parchment paper and drizzle the filling all over the dough. Gently spread it around with your hands or a rubber spatula until all the dough is covered.

7. Turn the parchment paper so that the short end of the dough is facing you. Starting with the short end closest to you, carefully use the parchment paper to start rolling the dough away from you into a tight roll. By using the paper, you eliminate uneven pressure from your hands, which will cause the dough to crack. If it cracks anyway, gently use your hands to mend it back together.

8. Once rolled, use a bread knife to cut the log into 6 evenly sized slices. Shape them into circles and place them cut side down on the prepared baking sheet, 1 inch apart.

9. Bake for 17 to 20 minutes, until they are nice and brown on the outside but still soft on the inside. Check them after 17 minutes.

10. Carefully place the cinnamon rolls on a plate and drizzle warm coconut butter over the top. Enjoy.

Fig Blueberry Jam

This jam spruces up lots of breakfast goodies, from pancakes to waffles to muffins. It goes well with the Rosemary Crackers (page 107) in the next chapter, too.

makes: **4 cups (1 L)** | prep time: **5 minutes** | cook time: **15 to 20 minutes**

Ingredients

2 cups (440 grams) fresh figs (see Note)

2 cups (260 grams) fresh or thawed frozen blueberries

½ cup (120 ml) organic honey

juice of 1 lemon

seeds from 1 vanilla bean (see Notes, page 87)

Process

1. Place the figs and blueberries in a blender or food processor and puree until smooth. (You can also use an immersion blender to puree the fruit in a medium saucepan, saving a cleaning step.)

2. Transfer the puree to a medium saucepan and add the honey, lemon juice, and vanilla bean seeds. Place over low heat and simmer for 15 to 20 minutes, stirring occasionally, until all the flavors have combined. Remove from the heat and let cool. Store in an airtight container in the refrigerator for up to 2 weeks.

note:

You can use dried figs after rehydrating them. Place 2 cups (300 grams) of dried figs in the bottom of a saucepan, pour in just enough water to cover the figs, and simmer over medium heat until the water is absorbed into the figs. It will take about 15 minutes. Remove from the heat, drain the water, and use as fresh figs in the recipe.

Blackberry Pear Jam

Like the Fig Blueberry Jam (page 101), this jam will get lots of use on your breakfast table—it is great as a topping for muffins, waffles, or pancakes, or smeared on Rosemary Crackers (page 107) for a quick snack.

makes: **3 cups (960 grams)** | prep time: **5 minutes** | cook time: **20 minutes**

Ingredients

1 cup (150 grams) diced pears (1 large pear)

2 cups (300 grams) fresh or thawed frozen blackberries

3 tablespoons organic honey

1 tablespoon freshly squeezed lemon juice

Process

1. Combine all the ingredients in a saucepan over medium heat. Once the blackberries begin to break down and the mixture turns a light purple color, use an immersion blender to puree. (Don't have an immersion blender? Pour the mixture into a blender and puree until smooth. Then return it to the saucepan.)

2. Simmer the pureed jam on low heat for 15 minutes. Remove from the heat and let rest for 10 minutes to set up. Store in an airtight container in the refrigerator for up to 2 weeks.

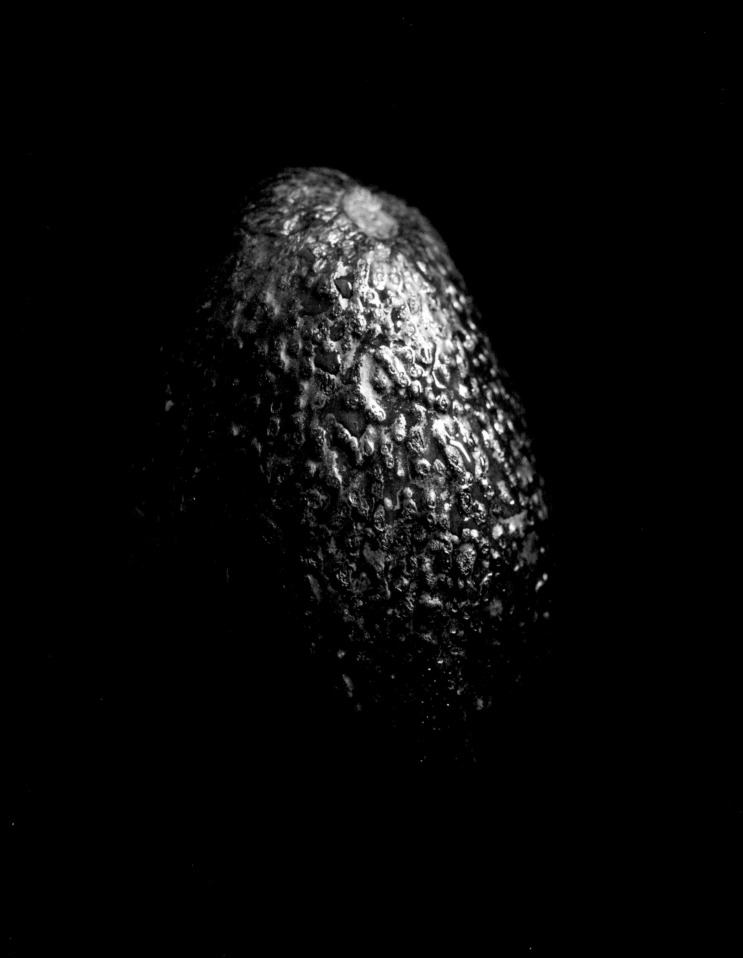

Starters & Snacks

Rosemary Crackers

makes: **20 (2-by-3-inch/5-by-7.5-cm) crackers** | prep time: **5 minutes** | cook time: **20 minutes**

Ingredients

2 cups (200 grams) blanched almond flour

½ teaspoon fine-grain sea salt

1 tablespoon dried rosemary, chopped

2 tablespoons water

1 large egg white

1 tablespoon extra virgin olive oil

¼ teaspoon coconut oil, melted

Process

1. Preheat the oven to 350°F (175°C).

2. Combine the almond flour, salt, and rosemary in a medium mixing bowl. In a small bowl, whisk together the water, egg white, olive oil, and coconut oil.

3. Pour the wet ingredients into the dry and stir until a stiff dough forms and all the dry ingredients are well incorporated.

4. Place the dough between 2 sheets of parchment paper and roll out to an even thickness of about ⅛ inch (3 mm).

5. Carefully transfer the parchment paper and dough to a baking sheet and remove the top piece of paper. Using a pizza cutter, trim off the uneven edges of the dough, then cut the sheet of dough into approximately 2-by-3-inch (5-by-7.5-cm) rectangles.

6. Bake for 10 minutes. Turn off the oven and let the crackers sit inside the oven for an additional 10 minutes, until golden.

Sweet Plantain Guacamole

serves: **4** I prep time: **15 minutes** I cook time: **10 minutes**

Ingredients

2 tablespoons coconut oil

4 cloves garlic, minced

1 large brown plantain, peeled and diced

2 tablespoons water

3 large avocados, cut in half and pitted

¼ medium white onion, finely chopped

handful of cilantro, roughly chopped

1 teaspoon minced jalapeño pepper

juice of ½ lime

¼ teaspoon smoked paprika

fine-grain sea salt and freshly ground pepper, to taste

Process

1. Place a small skillet over medium heat and add the coconut oil. Once the coconut oil is hot, add the garlic to the pan along with the diced plantain. When the plantain dice begin to brown, salt them, then flip to brown on the other side.

2. Add the water to the pan and cover to steam the plantain. Once the plantain dice are soft, remove from the heat and let cool.

3. While the plantain is steaming, scoop out the insides of the avocados and place in a large bowl. Mash up the avocado with a fork, then add the onion, cilantro, jalapeño, lime juice, smoked paprika, and salt and pepper. Mix well, then fold in the plantains. Chill in the refrigerator before serving.

Easy Guacamole

serves: **2 to 3** | prep time: **10 minutes**

Ingredients

2 avocados, cut in half and pitted

½ jalapeño pepper, minced (seed for less heat)

¼ small white onion, finely diced

2 cloves garlic, minced

½ teaspoon garlic powder

½ teaspoon cayenne pepper

juice of 1 lime

1 handful of fresh cilantro, roughly chopped

fine-grain sea salt and freshly ground black pepper, to taste

Process

Scoop out the insides of the avocados and place in a large bowl. Mash up the avocado with a fork. Add the rest of the ingredients and mix until well incorporated. Taste before serving to be sure it has enough salt. Serve cold.

Candied
Bacon

makes: **9 slices** I prep time: **5 minutes** I cook time: **30 to 35 minutes**

Ingredients

2 tablespoons coconut sugar

¼ cup (60 ml) maple syrup

9 slices bacon

Process

1. Preheat the oven to 350°F (175°C). Line a rimmed baking sheet with foil or parchment paper.

2. In a small bowl, mix together the coconut sugar and maple syrup. Lay the bacon flat on the prepared baking sheet. Use a pastry brush to brush the syrup mixture on top of the bacon. Bake for 30 to 35 minutes, or until the bacon is golden brown and slightly crispy.

3. Allow the bacon to cool on the baking sheet for 5 minutes before transferring to a serving plate to cool completely.

Pulled Pork Nachos

serves: **4 to 6 (or 2 to 3 as an entrée)** | prep time: **25 minutes** | cook time: **10 minutes**

Ingredients

3 small sweet potatoes or yams (about 14 ounces/400 grams), thinly sliced (see Note)

¼ cup (50 grams) coconut oil, melted

½ teaspoon plus 1 pinch coarse sea salt

4 ounces (115 grams) bacon, roughly chopped

1 pound (455 grams) leftover shredded Slow Cooker Pulled Pork (page 151)

¼ cup (120 grams) Easy Guacamole (page 111)

¼ cup (60 ml) Pico de Gallo (page 299)

¼ cup (60 ml) Tangy BBQ Sauce (page 303)

1 handful of fresh cilantro, roughly chopped, for garnish

Process

1. Preheat the oven to 425°F (218°C). Line a rimmed baking sheet with parchment paper.

2. Place the sliced sweet potatoes in a mixing bowl, pour the coconut oil over the top, and turn to coat the sweet potatoes in the oil. Sprinkle with ½ teaspoon of the salt.

3. Place the sweet potatoes on the prepared baking sheet, making sure not to overlap them. Bake for 25 minutes or until slightly browned.

4. While the sweet potatoes are roasting, cook the bacon in a medium cast-iron skillet over medium heat until more or less crispy (depending on your preference). Remove the pan from the heat and use a slotted spoon to transfer the bacon to a paper towel–lined plate to drain. Remove the bacon fat, leaving behind 1 tablespoon in the bottom of the skillet.

5. When the sweet potatoes are done, remove them from the oven and reduce the oven temperature to 350°F (175°C).

6. Line the bottom of the greased cast-iron skillet with half of the sweet potatoes. Then add half of the shredded pork on top. Repeat with the rest of the sweet potatoes and shredded pork. Sprinkle the bacon on top along with a pinch of salt. Place in the oven to bake for 10 minutes.

7. Serve topped with the guacamole, pico de gallo, and warm BBQ sauce. Finish with a sprinkling of chopped cilantro.

note:

We love sweet potato skin for its flavor, its texture, and the nutrition it adds to a meal. And because sometimes we are lazy. So, unless we're going for a smooth puree, we usually leave the skin on. If you don't like the skin, feel free to peel sweet potatoes for the recipes throughout this book—except for the loaded BBQ Sweet Potatoes (page 159). You gotta have the skin for that one.

Spinach & Artichoke Stuffed Portobello Mushrooms

serves: **4 to 5** | prep time: **20 minutes** | cook time: **15 minutes**

Ingredients

1 (16-ounce/455-gram) package frozen spinach, thawed and drained

2 (14-ounce/396-gram) cans quartered artichoke hearts, roughly chopped

coarse sea salt and freshly ground black pepper, to taste

1 cup (140 grams) roasted and unsalted cashews

3 tablespoons extra virgin olive oil

1 teaspoon garlic powder

1 teaspoon onion powder

½ teaspoon dried basil

¼ teaspoon cayenne pepper

4 or 5 portobello mushroom caps (about 12 ounces/340 grams), stems removed

Process

1. Preheat the oven to 350°F (175°C).

2. Combine the spinach and artichokes along with a sprinkle of salt in a large saucepan and set over medium heat to heat through.

3. Place the cashews in a food processor and grind until they have broken down into a texture similar to a coarse meal. Then add the olive oil, garlic and onion powders, basil, cayenne pepper, and salt and pepper and puree until smooth.

4. Add the cashew mixture to the saucepan with the spinach mixture and mix well. Reduce the heat to low and heat briefly to warm through. Fill the portobello mushroom caps with the filling. Place the mushroom caps on a rimmed baking sheet and bake for 15 minutes.

Avocado Caprese Stacks

makes: **8 stacks** | prep time: **10 minutes**

Ingredients

2 medium tomatoes

8 large fresh basil leaves

2 avocados, pitted and thinly sliced

pinch of coarse sea salt

balsamic vinegar, for garnish (optional)

Process

Cut the tomatoes into a total of 8 thick slices. Place a basil leaf on top of each tomato slice. Top with avocado slices and a pinch of salt. Sprinkle on some balsamic vinegar, if using.

Prosciutto Pears
with Balsamic Reduction

makes: **8 slices** | prep time: **5 minutes** | cook time: **45 minutes**

Ingredients

½ cup (120 ml) balsamic vinegar

1 large pear, cored and cut into 8 slices

4 slices prosciutto (2 ounces/55 grams), cut in half lengthwise

Process

1. In a small saucepan over medium heat, bring the vinegar to a boil, then reduce the heat to low and let thicken for 45 minutes.

2. Once the balsamic vinegar is reduced by half and is thick, wrap a slice of prosciutto around each slice of pear, then drizzle with the balsamic reduction.

Citrus Mint Sugar Salad

serves: 6 | prep time: 15 minutes

Ingredients

1 cup (10 grams) fresh mint leaves, plus extra for garnish

¼ cup (35 grams) coconut sugar

1 tablespoon water

1 teaspoon freshly squeezed lime juice

1 grapefruit, peeled and cut crosswise into ¼-inch (6-mm) rounds

2 oranges, peeled and cut crosswise into ¼-inch (6-mm) rounds

2 small blood oranges, peeled and cut crosswise into ¼-inch (6-mm) rounds

Process

1. Place the mint leaves and coconut sugar in a food processor or blender and blend until the mint leaves break down into the sugar. Place in a bowl, add the water and lime juice, and mix to combine.

2. Arrange the fruit on a platter, garnish with mint leaves, then pour the mint sugar sauce on top before serving.

Soups & Hearty Salads

Sage & Shallot Delicata Squash Soup

serves: **4** | prep time: **25 minutes** | cook time: **15 minutes**

Ingredients

2 delicata squash (about ¾ pound/340 grams)

2 tablespoons coconut oil

2 shallots (1¾ ounces/50 grams), thinly sliced

2 cloves garlic, thinly sliced

2 cups (480 ml) chicken broth

2 tablespoons roughly chopped fresh sage, plus 4 to 8 sage leaves for garnish (optional)

pinch of coarse sea salt and freshly ground black pepper, to taste

Process

1. Preheat the oven to 400°F (205°C).

2. Cut the delicata squash in half lengthwise and place cut side down on a baking sheet. Bake for 25 minutes, or until soft. Use a spoon to remove the seeds, discard them, and then scoop out the flesh of the squash and place it in a bowl.

3. Heat the coconut oil in a large saucepan over medium heat. Add the shallots and garlic and cook, stirring often, until the shallots are soft. Add the delicata squash, broth, sage, and salt and pepper and mix to combine.

4. Using an immersion blender, blend together until smooth. Taste and add more salt if needed, blending once more to mix in the salt. Garnish each bowl of soup with one or two fresh sage leaves, if desired.

Creamy Cauliflower Soup

serves: **6** | prep time: **10 minutes** | cook time: **1 hour 10 minutes**

Ingredients

1 large head cauliflower (about 2¼ pounds/1 kg), cut into florets

¼ cup (50 grams) coconut oil, melted, divided

¼ teaspoon coarse sea salt, plus more to taste

1 large sweet onion, sliced

4 cloves garlic, sliced

2 cups (480 ml) chicken broth

1 cup water (240 ml)

1 (14-ounce/415-ml) can full-fat coconut milk

freshly ground black pepper, to taste

¼ cup (30 grams) halved pecans, for garnish

½ red bell pepper, diced, for garnish

1 teaspoon olive oil, for garnish (optional)

Process

1. Preheat the oven to 450°F (230°C). Line a rimmed baking sheet with parchment paper.

2. Place the cauliflower in a large bowl, drizzle with 2 tablespoons of the coconut oil, and sprinkle in the salt. Toss to coat.

3. Arrange the cauliflower in a single layer on the prepared baking sheet. Bake for 40 minutes, or until tender and browned, stirring once after 25 minutes.

4. Heat the remaining 2 tablespoons of coconut oil in a Dutch oven over medium heat. Add the onion and garlic and sauté for 5 minutes, stirring occasionally. Add the cauliflower, broth, and water and bring to a boil.

5. Reduce the heat to low and simmer for 20 minutes, stirring occasionally. Remove from the heat and stir in the coconut milk and salt and pepper to taste. Using an immersion blender, puree the soup until smooth. Serve in soup bowls and garnish with the pecans and red peppers. If desired, finish the soup with dots of olive oil on top.

Crock-Pot
French Onion Soup

serves: 4 | prep time: **10 minutes** | cook time: **3 to 4 hours +**
6 to 8 hours if caramelizing the onions

Ingredients

2 or 4 tablespoons bacon fat or coconut oil, melted (see Note)

3 pounds (1.4 kg) onions, sliced

2 cups (180 ml) chicken broth

4 cups (960 ml) beef broth

6 sprigs fresh thyme

3 sprigs fresh rosemary

3 bay leaves

2 teaspoons coarse sea salt, plus more if needed

2 teaspoons freshly ground black pepper

Process

1. Grease the inside of a slow cooker with 2 tablespoons of the bacon fat or coconut oil.

2. If you're not caramelizing the onions, skip ahead to the next step. Otherwise, place the onions in the slow cooker and pour the remaining 2 tablespoons of bacon fat or coconut oil over the top of the onions. Cover and cook on high for 6 to 8 hours, stirring every 2 hours while the onions caramelize.

3. If you have not caramelized the onions, add the raw onions to the greased slow cooker. Add the chicken broth, beef broth, thyme, rosemary, bay leaves, salt, and pepper and mix well. Cover and cook on high for 3 to 4 hours. Taste the soup and add additional salt to taste if needed. Remove the herbs from the soup before serving.

note:

Caramelizing the onions for this recipe is optional, but it enhances the flavor. If you're caramelizing them, you will need 4 tablespoons melted bacon fat or coconut oil; if you're not caramelizing them, 2 tablespoons is sufficient.

Pumpkin Tomato Soup

serves: 6 | prep time: **10 minutes** | cook time: **35 minutes**

Ingredients

2 tablespoons coconut oil

1 medium onion, diced

coarse sea salt and freshly ground black pepper, to taste

2 (15-ounce/425-gram) cans pumpkin puree

1 teaspoon dried thyme

1 (14.5-ounce/411-gram) can diced tomatoes

2 cups (480 ml) chicken broth

1 cinnamon stick

½ teaspoon freshly grated nutmeg

¼ cup (60 ml) organic honey

½ cup (120 ml) full-fat coconut milk

½ cup (60 grams) toasted salted pumpkin seeds, for garnish

Process

1. Heat the coconut oil in a medium stockpot or Dutch oven over medium heat. Add the onion and a pinch of salt and cook until tender and translucent, about 5 minutes. Add the pumpkin, thyme, tomatoes, chicken broth, cinnamon stick, nutmeg, and honey and bring to a simmer.

2. Reduce the heat to medium-low and let simmer for 30 minutes, then remove the cinnamon stick and add the coconut milk. Use an immersion blender to puree the soup, or transfer in small batches to a blender to puree. Season to taste with salt and pepper, and blend once more. Garnish with the toasted pumpkin seeds and serve.

Squash Medley Lavender Soup

SOUPS &
HEARTY
SALADS

serves: **4** | prep time: **15 minutes** | cook time: **1 hour**

Ingredients

3 to 4 tablespoons coconut oil, melted, divided

1 butternut squash (about 1¾ pounds/800 grams), cut in half lengthwise

1 acorn squash (about ¾ pound/340 grams), cut in half crosswise

1 delicata squash (about 9 ounces/255 grams), cut in half lengthwise

½ cup (120 ml) full-fat coconut milk

2 tablespoons maple syrup

1 tablespoon dried lavender buds, plus extra for garnish (optional)

coarse sea salt and freshly ground black pepper, to taste

Process

1. Preheat the oven to 375°F (190°C). Line a rimmed baking sheet with aluminum foil.

2. Using 1 to 2 tablespoons of the coconut oil, brush the cut sides of the squash. Place cut side down on the prepared baking sheet and roast in the oven until all the squash is fork-tender, 25 to 50 minutes. (Different sizes of squash will finish cooking at different times, so you may need to remove the smaller squash and let the larger squash continue cooking.)

3. Remove all the squash from the oven and let cool slightly. Use a spoon to scrape out and discard all the seeds and the excess strings. Then scrape out the flesh of the squash and place it in a food processor or blender.

4. Add the remaining 2 tablespoons of coconut oil, coconut milk, maple syrup, and lavender and process until silky and smooth. Add salt and pepper to taste and pulse once more. Pour into bowls, garnish with lavender buds if desired, and serve.

notes:

You can use any combination of squash you want, as long as the total weight equals about 3 pounds (1.4 kg), or 3 cups (1.3 kg) once roasted and mashed. You can make the soup thinner if desired by adding water, broth (any kind), or more coconut milk.

Chicken Zoodle Soup

serves: **8** | prep time: **10 minutes** | cook time: **30 minutes**

Ingredients

2 quarts (2 L) chicken or vegetable broth

1 small onion, diced

2 carrots, peeled and sliced

3 stalks celery, diced

2 sprigs fresh thyme

1 small zucchini (about 10 ounces/280 grams), cut into "zoodles" (see Note)

2 cups (300 grams) shredded, leftover Lemon Rosemary Roasted Chicken (page 193)

coarse sea salt and freshly ground black pepper, to taste

Process

Bring the broth to a boil in a large stockpot and then reduce to a simmer. Add the onion, carrots, celery, and thyme to the pot, cover, and simmer for 15 to 20 minutes, or until the vegetables are tender. Add the zucchini noodles, shredded chicken, and salt and pepper to the pot and simmer for 5 to 10 more minutes. Turn off the heat and serve immediately.

note:

To make "zoodles," use a julienne peeler to cut the zucchini into long noodle-like strands. You can also use a spiral slicer.

Savory
Beef Chili

serves: **8** | prep time: **10 minutes** | cook time: **8 hours**

Ingredients

2 pounds (910 grams) ground beef

1 yellow onion, diced

1 red bell pepper, seeded and diced

1 yellow bell pepper, seeded and diced

4 cloves garlic, minced

1 (14.5-ounce/411-gram) can diced tomatoes

1 (8-ounce/225-gram) can tomato sauce

1 (20-ounce/565-gram) can crushed pineapple, juices drained

2 tablespoons chili powder

3 tablespoons paprika

1 tablespoon ground cumin

1 teaspoon cayenne pepper

2 teaspoons coarse sea salt

1 teaspoon freshly ground black pepper

Process

1. Place the ground beef, onion, bell peppers, garlic, diced tomatoes, tomato sauce, and crushed pineapple in a slow cooker and stir well, breaking up the ground beef as much as possible. Add the chili powder, paprika, cumin, cayenne, salt, and pepper and mix well.

2. Cover and cook on low for 8 hours. Once done, stir well before serving.

note:

For added flavor, you can brown the ground beef in a sauté pan over medium-high heat before placing it in the slow cooker.

Steak
Fajita Salad

serves: **4** | prep time: **1 to 24 hours** | cook time: **20 minutes**

Ingredients

For the wet rub

2 tablespoons coconut oil, melted

juice of 1 lime

1 tablespoon smoked paprika

½ tablespoon chili powder

1 teaspoon garlic powder

1 teaspoon onion powder

1 teaspoon coarse sea salt

½ teaspoon ground cumin

½ teaspoon dried ground oregano

1 pound (455 grams) flank steak

2 tablespoons coconut oil, melted

1 red onion, thinly sliced

1 red bell pepper, seeded and thinly sliced

1 orange bell pepper, seeded and thinly sliced

2 cups (150 grams) button mushrooms, sliced

coarse sea salt and freshly ground black pepper, to taste

2 romaine hearts

lime wedges, for garnish

Avocado Mousse, for garnish (page 297)

Process

1. In a large bowl, combine the ingredients for the wet rub, mixing them together well. Add the steak to the bowl and rub the paste all over, massaging it into the meat. Cover the bowl and set it in the fridge to marinate for a minimum of 1 hour and a maximum of 24 hours. Once the steak is done marinating, thinly slice it against the grain into pieces ½ inch (12 mm) wide.

2. Heat the coconut oil in a large sauté pan over medium heat. Add the onion and bell peppers and cook until the onion becomes translucent, approximately 4 to 5 minutes, then add the mushrooms and mix well. Sprinkle with salt and pepper and cook until the mushrooms have browned, about 3 minutes.

3. While the vegetables are cooking, preheat a cast-iron skillet over high heat. (You may need to grease the pan if it is not well seasoned.) Once the pan is hot, sear the steak slices, making sure to not crowd the pan. Cook for a total of 2 to 3 minutes for medium doneness. Repeat with all the steak. Once the steak is cooked, add the slices to the pan with the vegetables and toss to mix together.

4. Chop up the romaine hearts and divide among 4 plates, then top with the fajita mixture. Serve with lime wedges on the side and a dollop of avocado mousse on top (or, for a fancier presentation, pipe the mousse on top using a piping bag or a plastic bag with the corner snipped).

Creamy Pesto
Chicken Salad

serves: **2** | prep time: **5 minutes**

Ingredients

⅓ **cup (75 ml) 30-Second Mayo (page 290)**

3 tablespoons Pistachio Pesto (page 293)

1½ cups (200 grams) shredded leftover Lemon Rosemary Roasted Chicken (page 193)

¼ **cup (30 grams) minced red onion**

coarse sea salt and freshly ground black pepper, to taste

avocado slices, for serving

tomato slices, for serving

Process

In a bowl, mix together the mayo and pistachio pesto. Add the chicken and red onion and season with salt and pepper. Mix well to evenly coat the chicken with the mayo. Serve the chicken salad with avocado and tomato slices.

Cranberry Chicken Salad

serves: **2** | prep time: **10 minutes**

Ingredients

1½ cups (200 grams) shredded leftover Honey Mustard Chicken Thighs (page 189)

½ cup (70 grams) cranberries

½ cup (50 grams) shredded carrots

¼ cup (25 grams) diced green apple

⅓ cup (75 ml) 30-Second Mayo (page 290)

½ cup (60 grams) crushed, raw pecans

4 large tomato slices, for serving

coarse sea salt and freshly ground black pepper, to taste

Process

1. Place all the ingredients except the tomato slices and salt and pepper in a bowl and mix well.

2. Set a slice of tomato on a plate, mound half of the chicken salad on top of it, then lay another slice of tomato on top of the chicken salad. Sprinkle with salt and pepper and repeat with the remaining tomato slices and chicken salad.

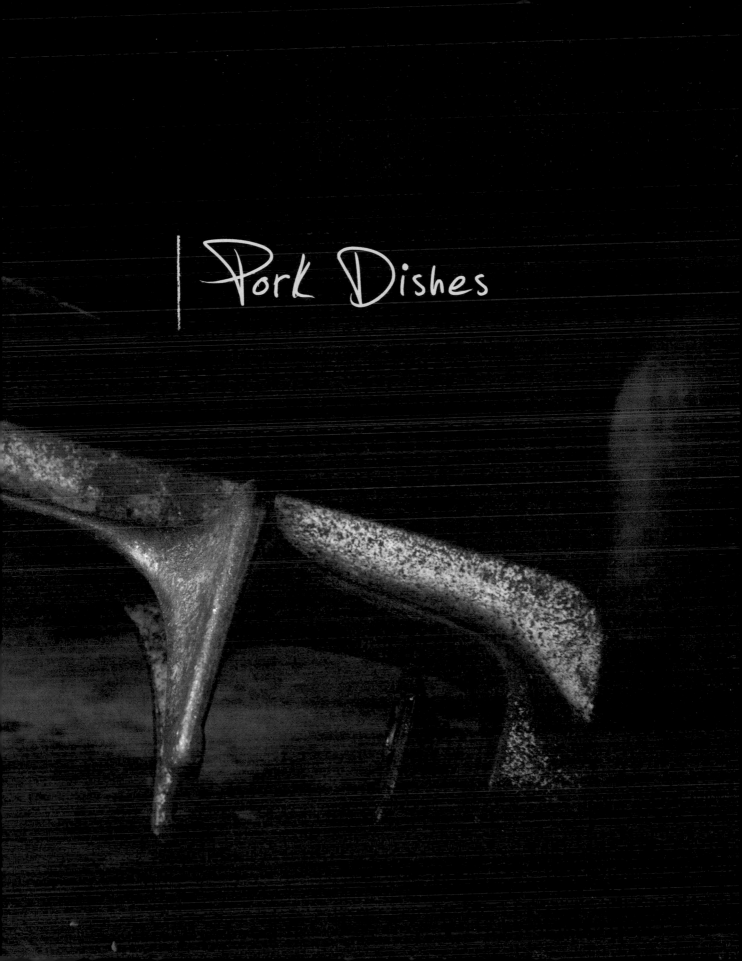

Pork Dishes

Pan-Seared Rosemary Sage
Pork Chops with Apples & Pears

serves: **2** | prep time: **5 minutes** | cook time: **25 to 35 minutes**

Ingredients

2 bone-in pork chops (1 pound/455 grams)

coarse sea salt and freshly ground black pepper, to taste

2 Fuji apples, cored and sliced

2 pears, cored and sliced

4 sprigs fresh rosemary

4 sprigs fresh sage

Process

1. Preheat the oven to 200°F (95°C).

2. Heat a 12-inch (30.5-cm) cast-iron skillet over high heat. Season the pork chops liberally with salt and pepper on each side. Once the pan is very hot, place both of the pork chops in the pan and sear for 90 seconds on each side.

3. After both sides of the pork chops have been seared, remove the chops from the pan and set aside. Line the bottom of the cast-iron skillet with a layer of apples and pears. Next, layer the rosemary and sage sprigs on top of the apples and pears.

4. Place the pork chops on top of the herbs and fruit, insert a leave-in meat thermometer (if you have one) in a pork chop, and place the skillet in the oven. Cook for 25 to 35 minutes, or until the internal temperature of the pork chops reaches a minimum of 140°F (60°C).

Slow Cooker
Pulled Pork

serves: **4** | prep time: **3 to 48 hours** | cook time: **8 to 10 hours**

Ingredients

For the spice rub

2 tablespoons smoked paprika

1 tablespoon coarse sea salt

1 tablespoon chili powder

1 tablespoon ground cumin

½ tablespoon freshly ground black pepper

½ tablespoon dried ground oregano

½ tablespoon ground white pepper

1 teaspoon cayenne pepper

2 pounds (910 grams) bone-in pork shoulder

¼ cup (60 ml) water

Process

1. In a small mixing bowl, combine all the ingredients for the spice rub and mix well.

2. Massage the spice rub all over the meat. Wrap tightly in a double layer of plastic wrap and refrigerate for at least 3 hours and up to 48 hours.

3. Unwrap the meat and place it in a slow cooker. Add the water and turn the slow cooker to low. Cook for 8 to 10 hours, until the meat is fork-tender.

4. With the pork still in the slow cooker, use 2 forks to pull it apart.

Twice-Baked Stuffed Butternut Squash

serves: **4** | prep time: **10 minutes** | cook time: **50 minutes**

Ingredients

1 butternut squash (about 2 pounds/910 grams), cut in half lengthwise

1 tablespoon coconut oil

½ small yellow onion, diced

1 apple, cored and diced

1 pound (455 grams) ground pork

2 teaspoons dried parsley

⅛ teaspoon ground cinnamon

1 teaspoon coarse sea salt

½ teaspoon freshly ground black pepper

1 tablespoon blanched almond flour

Process

1. Preheat the oven to 400°F (205°C). Line a rimmed baking sheet with parchment paper.

2. Place the butternut squash cut side down on the prepared baking sheet. Place in the oven and bake for 30 minutes, or until the squash is soft to the touch. Remove from the oven and let the squash cool. Turn the oven down to 350°F (175°C).

3. While the butternut squash cools, heat the coconut oil in a large sauté pan over medium heat. Add the diced onion and apple and sauté until the onion is translucent. Add the ground pork, parsley, cinnamon, salt, and pepper. Cook, breaking apart the meat with a spatula, until no pink remains, about 10 minutes.

4. Remove and discard the seeds from the butternut squash, then scoop out the flesh and place in a bowl, leaving behind ¼ inch (6 mm) of flesh to keep from tearing the skin. Mash the squash with a fork and place it in the pan with the ground pork. Mix until well combined.

5. Place the hollowed-out squash halves in a large baking dish. Fill with the pork mixture and sprinkle the almond flour on top. Bake for 10 minutes. Serve immediately.

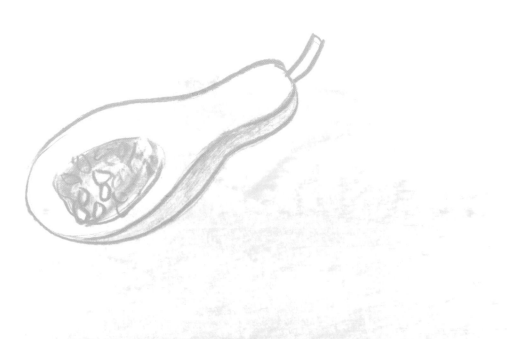

Perfect Ribs

serves: **4** | prep time: **15 minutes** | cook time: **5 hours (smoker)**
or **2 hours (oven)** or **8 hours (slow cooker)**

Ingredients

For the BBQ rub

2 tablespoons smoked paprika

1 tablespoon coarse sea salt

1 tablespoon chili powder

1 tablespoon ground cumin

2 teaspoons freshly ground black pepper

2 teaspoons dried ground oregano

2 teaspoons ground white pepper

1 teaspoon cayenne pepper

For the ribs

8 pounds (3.6 kg) baby back ribs

¼ cup (60 ml) yellow mustard

¼ cup (60 ml) olive oil

¼ cup (60 ml) apple juice

Blueberry BBQ Sauce (page 301), for serving

Process

1. Combine all the spices for the BBQ rub in a small bowl and mix well.

2. Remove the membrane from the ribs. This is the thin skin on the bone or concave side of the rack. To remove it, insert a table knife under the membrane along the bone end and slide it back and forth to loosen the membrane. Grab the slippery membrane with a paper towel and lift it off.

3. Rinse the ribs under cold water and pat dry. Place on a clean work surface and lightly coat each rack of ribs, top and bottom, with the yellow mustard (this will be the seasoning glue). Generously season the ribs on the top and bottom with the BBQ rub, covering the entire surface of the meat with the seasoning. At this point, you can cover the ribs and place them in the refrigerator to let those flavors penetrate the meat for 4 to 24 hours, or you can cook them right away.

4. Mix together the olive oil and apple juice and set aside. This will be used to baste the ribs while cooking.

Smoker Method

1. Preheat the smoker to 200°F (95°C) and try to maintain that temperature.

2. Place the ribs, bone side down, in the smoker and smoke for 3 hours. Once 3 hours have elapsed, remove the ribs from the smoker and individually wrap each rack of ribs with aluminum foil.

3. Before closing the foil, generously apply the olive oil and apple juice mixture to each rack of ribs. Seal the foil so that no liquid leaks out. Place the ribs back in the smoker and let cook for another 2 hours.

4. Remove from the smoker and let the ribs rest for about 10 minutes. Remove from the foil, slice the ribs, and serve with the Blueberry BBQ Sauce.

Oven Method

1. Line a rimmed baking sheet with aluminum foil and then place a wire rack on top of the sheet. Lay the ribs on the rack in a single layer, meaty side up.

2. Turn on the broiler to high and place the ribs a few inches below the broiler for 5 minutes to brown the meaty side.

3. Set the oven temperature to 300°F (150°C) and move the ribs to the middle rack of the oven. Cook the ribs for 1 hour.

4. Remove the ribs from the oven, wrap each rack individually with aluminum foil, and generously apply the olive oil and apple juice mixture to each rack before sealing the aluminum foil.

5. Place the ribs back in the oven to finish cooking for another 30 to 45 minutes. Remove the ribs from the oven and let them rest for about 10 minutes, covered. Uncover, slice the ribs, and serve with the Blueberry BBQ Sauce.

Slow Cooker Method

1. Place the ribs in a slow cooker. Drizzle the olive oil and apple juice mixture over the top of all the ribs. Cover and cook on low for 6 to 8 hours.

2. Once done, gently remove the ribs from the slow cooker and place on an aluminum foil–lined rimmed baking sheet. Broil under a broiler set to high heat for 3 to 5 minutes to brown the ribs. Remove from the oven, slice the ribs, and serve with Blueberry BBQ Sauce.

Shredded Pork Meatloaf

serves: **6 to 8** | prep time: **5 minutes** | cook time: **30 minutes**

Ingredients

1 pound (455 grams) ground beef

1 pound (455 grams) shredded leftover Slow Cooker Pulled Pork (page 151)

1 small yellow onion, diced

2 teaspoons garlic powder

2 teaspoons smoked paprika

1 teaspoon chili powder

coarse sea salt and freshly ground black pepper, to taste

coconut oil, for greasing the loaf pan

½ to 1 cup (120 to 240 ml) Tangy BBQ Sauce (page 303)

Process

1. Preheat the oven to 400°F (205°C).

2. Place all the ingredients, except the BBQ sauce, in a large bowl and mix well.

3. Grease a 9-by-5-inch (23-by-13-cm) loaf pan with coconut oil. Put the beef and pork mixture in the loaf pan and press down to even out the top.

4. Bake for 30 minutes, or until the top of the meatloaf is nicely browned.

5. While the meatloaf bakes, make the BBQ sauce. After removing the meatloaf from the oven, top with warm BBQ sauce and let rest in the pan for 5 minutes before serving.

Loaded BBQ
Sweet Potatoes

serves: **2 to 4** | prep time: **35 minutes** | cook time: **10 minutes**

Ingredients

4 small sweet potatoes or yams (1+ pound/455+ grams)

1½ cups (340 grams) shredded leftover Perfect Ribs (page 154)

½ cup (120 ml) Tangy BBQ Sauce (page 303)

⅓ cup (35 grams) shredded carrots

⅓ cup (25 grams) shredded green cabbage

¼ cup (30 grams) chopped red onion

⅓ cup (75 ml) 30-Second Mayo (page 290)

Process

1. Preheat the oven to 400°F (205°C).

2. Use a fork to poke holes in the sweet potatoes or yams. Place in the oven on a rimmed baking sheet and bake for 35 minutes. Remove from the oven and reduce the temperature to 350°F (175°C).

3. After you've removed the sweet potatoes or yams from the oven, mix together the shredded pork ribs and BBQ sauce until the meat is well coated.

4. Cut each sweet potato or yam down the middle and open them up. In the middle of each sweet potato, add a little over ¼ cup (60 g) of the sauced shredded ribs. Place back in the oven and bake for 10 minutes, or until the shredded ribs are heated through.

5. While the stuffed sweet potatoes bake, mix together the carrots, cabbage, red onion, and mayo in a small bowl. Top the stuffed sweet potatoes with the cabbage mixture.

Asian Cabbage Slaw
Pork Burgers

serves: **4** | prep time: **10 minutes** | cook time: **10 to 12 minutes**

Ingredients

For the burgers

1⅓ pounds (606 grams) ground pork

1½ teaspoons garlic powder

generous pinch of coarse sea salt

For the cabbage slaw

1 cup (50 grams) thinly sliced red cabbage

1 cup (50 grams) thinly sliced yellow cabbage

1 cup (60 grams) thinly sliced carrots

½ green apple, thinly sliced

2 tablespoons coconut aminos

juice of 1 lime

1 teaspoon sesame oil

½ teaspoon organic honey

½ teaspoon sesame seeds

¼ teaspoon finely grated fresh ginger

2 tablespoons chopped green onions, plus 1 tablespoon sliced green onions for garnish (optional)

¼ cup (35 grams) unsalted roasted cashews, roughly chopped

fine-grain sea salt and freshly ground black pepper, to taste

Process

1. Preheat the grill to medium-high heat.

2. In a large bowl, mix together the ground pork, garlic powder, and salt. Form into 4 patties.

3. Grill the burgers on each side for 5 to 6 minutes, until cooked to an internal temperature of 160°F (71°C). After you've flipped the burgers, make the cabbage slaw.

4. In a large bowl, mix together all the ingredients for the slaw. Serve the burgers on top of the slaw. Garnish with sliced green onions, if desired.

Perfect Meatballs with Sage Sweet Potato Noodles

serves: **4** | prep time: **10 minutes** | cook time: **25 minutes**

Ingredients

3 sweet potatoes (1⅓ pound/600 grams), peeled

4 tablespoons coconut oil, divided

2 tablespoons minced fresh sage, divided

1 tablespoon fresh rosemary, minced, divided

1 teaspoon coarse sea salt

1 teaspoon freshly ground black pepper

½ pound (225 grams) ground beef

½ pound (225 grams) ground pork

½ teaspoon garlic powder

Process

1. Using a spiral slicer, cut the sweet potatoes into noodles.

2. Heat 2 tablespoons of the coconut oil in a large sauté pan over medium-low heat. Add the noodles along with 1 tablespoon of the sage, ½ tablespoon of the rosemary, the salt, and the pepper. Toss the noodles to coat them in the coconut oil and let them cook down for 10 to 15 minutes, stirring every couple of minutes to keep them from sticking. When the noodles are soft and slightly browned, remove the pan from the heat.

3. Preheat the oven to 350°F (175°C).

4. In a large bowl, mix together the ground beef, ground pork, remaining 1 tablespoon of sage, remaining ½ tablespoon of rosemary, the garlic powder, and a pinch of salt and pepper. Use a large cookie scoop or ice cream scoop to form the meat into 18 meatballs.

5. Heat the remaining 2 tablespoons of coconut oil in a large cast-iron skillet (or oven-safe skillet) over medium-high heat. Add the meatballs and cook on all sides for 2 to 3 minutes, until they are slightly browned. Transfer the meatballs to a 9-by-13-inch (22-by-33-cm) baking dish and bake for 10 minutes. Serve the meatballs over the cooked sweet potato noodles.

note:

If you don't own a spiral slicer, grate the sweet potatoes or cut them into julienne strips.

Beef Dishes

Sweet & Savory
Open-Faced Sliders

makes: **9 sliders** | prep time: **30 minutes** | cook time: **10 minutes**

Ingredients

1 sweet potato, about 2 inches (5 cm) in diameter

4 tablespoons coconut oil, melted, divided

¼ cup (60 ml) Maple Mayo (page 290)

1 pound (455 grams) ground beef

¼ yellow onion, minced

1 clove garlic, minced

½ teaspoon coarse sea salt

¼ teaspoon freshly ground black pepper

9 slices prosciutto (5 ounces/140 grams)

1 pear, cored and diced

Process

1. Preheat the oven to 400°F (205°C). Line a rimmed baking sheet with aluminum foil.

2. Cut the sweet potato into 9 rounds ½ inch (12 mm) thick.

3. In a large bowl, coat the sweet potato rounds in 2 tablespoons of the coconut oil.

4. Place the sweet potato rounds on the prepared baking sheet. Bake the rounds for 30 minutes. While the sweet potatoes are baking, make the maple mayo and place in the refrigerator to chill.

5. Preheat the grill to medium heat.

6. In a large bowl, mix together the ground beef, onion, garlic, salt, and pepper. Create 9 small patties and press your thumb into the middle of each patty to create a dimple. (This will keep the patties from puffing up in the middle while cooking.)

7. Place the patties on the grill grate and grill, covered, for about 4 minutes per side. Let rest after cooking.

8. While the patties are cooking, heat a skillet over medium heat. Add the prosciutto to the hot pan one slice at a time and cook for only 5 seconds per side, just to slightly cook the prosciutto.

9. In the same hot pan, add the remaining 2 tablespoons of coconut oil and the diced pear. Cook until slightly browned.

10. Stack the sliders in this order: sweet potato round, burger patty, 1 teaspoon maple mayo, slice of prosciutto, and 1 teaspoon of diced pear on top.

Four-Layer Beef & Bacon Casserole

serves: **8** | prep time: **1 hour 10 minutes** | cook time: **35 minutes**

Ingredients

coconut oil, for greasing the baking dish

½ pound (225 grams) bacon, for garnish

For the sweet potato mash

3 to 4 medium sweet potatoes (1¼ pounds/560 grams)

¼ cup (60 ml) full-fat coconut milk

½ teaspoon dried sage

¼ teaspoon coarse sea salt

¼ teaspoon freshly ground black pepper

For the cauliflower mash

1 head cauliflower (about 1½ pounds/750 grams), cut into florets

¼ cup (60 ml) coconut milk

½ teaspoon coarse sea salt

1 teaspoon freshly ground black pepper

For the ground beef mixture

2 pounds (910 grams) ground beef

1 clove garlic, minced

1 medium yellow onion, diced

8 ounces (225 grams) button mushrooms, diced

1 teaspoon coarse sea salt

½ teaspoon freshly ground black pepper

Process

1. Preheat the oven to 375°F (190°C). Grease a 9-by-13-inch (23-by-33-cm) baking dish.

2. Place the bacon on a rimmed baking sheet and bake in the oven for 12 to 15 minutes, or until cooked through. Roughly chop the bacon. Set aside.

3. Turn up the oven to 400°F (205°C). Poke holes in the sweet potatoes with a fork. Place on a rimmed baking sheet and bake for 35 to 40 minutes, or until the sweet potatoes are soft and easily pierced with a knife. The time may range depending on the thickness of the sweet potatoes.

4. While the potatoes are baking, steam the cauliflower. Once the cauliflower is fork-tender, place it in a food processor or blender and puree until it becomes soft and resembles mashed potatoes. Add the coconut milk, salt, and pepper and continue to blend until smooth. Remove from the blender and set aside. Clean out the food processor or blender for the sweet potato mash.

5. When the sweet potatoes are soft, remove their skins and place the sweet potatoes in the clean food processor or blender. Blend until the sweet potatoes break down, then add the coconut milk, sage, salt, and pepper and puree until smooth. Set aside for later.

6. Cook the ground beef in a large sauté pan or Dutch oven over medium-high heat, breaking it apart with a wooden spoon. Once the meat begins to brown, add the garlic, onion, and mushrooms. Sprinkle with the salt and pepper and continue to cook until the meat is cooked through, then remove the pan from the heat.

7. Create the layers: Use a slotted spoon to remove half of the meat mixture from the excess liquid in the pan and place in the prepared baking dish in one layer. Then pour the cauliflower mash mixture on top of the meat and spread it out. Then, using the slotted spoon, add the other half of the meat on top of the cauliflower mash. Lastly, pour the sweet potato mash on top and spread it evenly.

8. Turn the oven down to 350°F (175°C). Place the casserole in the oven and bake for 30 minutes, or until it begins to bubble. Then turn on the broiler to high and cook for 5 minutes to brown the top of the casserole. Let rest to thicken and garnish with the bacon before serving.

Bacon Beef Stew

serves: **6** | prep time: **10 minutes** | cook time: **8 hours**

Ingredients

4 slices bacon, cut crosswise into lardons ¼ inch (6 mm) thick

4 large carrots, peeled and cut into chunks

1 (16-ounce/455-gram) package frozen pearl onions

4 to 8 ounces (115 to 225 grams) crimini mushrooms, diced

1 cup (70 grams) shredded red cabbage

4 cloves garlic, minced

2 pounds (910 grams) stew meat

1 teaspoon coarse sea salt

1 teaspoon freshly ground black pepper

2 (14.5-ounce/415-gram) cans diced fire-roasted tomatoes

1 (8-ounce/225-gram) can tomato sauce

1 green onion, sliced, for garnish

Process

1. In a sauté pan over medium heat, cook the bacon lardons until brown, about 10 minutes.

2. While the bacon is cooking, place the carrots, onions, mushrooms, cabbage, and garlic in the bottom of a slow cooker. Add the stew meat along with the salt and pepper. Then add the tomatoes and tomato sauce and mix it all together. Pour the bacon and all the bacon fat on top and mix once more.

3. Cover and cook on low for 8 hours. Ladle into bowls and garnish with the sliced green onion.

Marinated Steak & Pineapple Kabobs

serves: **4** | prep time: **6 to 24 hours** | cook time: **10 minutes**

Ingredients

1 cup (240 ml) olive oil

½ cup (120 ml) coconut aminos

½ cup (120 ml) freshly squeezed lemon juice

¼ cup (60 ml) Dijon mustard

2 cloves garlic, minced

¼ cup (60 ml) organic honey

1 teaspoon freshly ground black pepper

2 pounds (910 grams) tender cut of beef, such as sirloin or filet, cut into 2-inch (5-cm) cubes

1 large yellow bell pepper, seeded and cut into large chunks

1 large red bell pepper, seeded and cut into large chunks

1 large orange bell pepper, seeded and cut into large chunks

1 medium yellow onion, cut into large chunks

2 cups (360 grams) pineapple chunks (about ½ small pineapple)

Process

1. In a large resealable bag, combine the olive oil, coconut aminos, lemon juice, mustard, garlic, honey, black pepper, and beef. Seal and place in the refrigerator to marinate for 6 to 24 hours.

2. About ½ hour before you plan to cook the meat, preheat the grill to medium heat.

3. Use metal or wooden skewers (see Note) to create the kabobs: Place the peppers, onions, marinated meat, and pineapple onto skewers in any order.

4. Place the skewers on the grill grate and grill for 5 minutes with the lid closed. Flip the skewers over and cook for another 3 to 5 minutes for medium, or longer if you prefer more well-done meat. Remove from the grill and serve.

note:

If you use wooden or bamboo skewers, soak them in water for half an hour before putting them on the grill.

Carne Asada

serves: **4 to 6** | prep time: **4 to 48 hours** | cook time: **8 minutes**

Ingredients

2 pounds (910 grams) flank or skirt steak

coarse sea salt and freshly ground black pepper

For the marinade

4 cloves garlic, minced

½ red onion, minced

1 jalapeño pepper, seeded and minced

1 teaspoon ground cumin

1 large handful fresh cilantro, leaves and stems finely chopped

pinch of coarse sea salt and freshly ground black pepper

juice of 1 lime

juice of 1 lemon

juice of 1 orange

½ cup (120 ml) olive oil

Process

1. Lay the flank steak in a glass baking dish or other nonreactive container.

2. In a bowl, combine all the marinade ingredients. Pour the marinade over the steak, making sure each piece is well coated. Cover and refrigerate for at least 4 hours and up to 48 hours.

3. Preheat the grill to medium-high heat. Remove the steak from the marinade, season both sides generously with salt and pepper, and place on the grill grate.

4. Grill for 2 to 3 minutes on each side, depending on how thin the meat is, or to your preference. Thin pieces can fully cook in under 2 minutes. Do not overcook.

5. Remove the steak and let rest for 5 minutes. Slice thinly against the grain and serve.

Garlic & Thyme Standing Rib Roast

serves: **6** | prep time: **5 minutes** | cook time: **60 to 90 minutes**

Ingredients

For the paste

4 cloves garlic, peeled

pinch of coarse sea salt

2 tablespoons fresh thyme leaves, minced

1 tablespoon freshly ground black pepper

¼ cup (60 ml) olive oil

4 pounds (1.8 kg) bone-in standing rib roast

coarse sea salt

Process

1. Preheat the oven to 450°F (230°C).

2. Using a chef's knife, finely chop the garlic and sprinkle on a small pinch of salt. Continue chopping to work the salt throughout the garlic, then, using the side of your knife held at a 20-degree angle to the board, drag the garlic across the surface of the cutting board while applying pressure. The salt acts as an abrasive and helps break the garlic down into a paste. Using the back edge (not the cutting edge) of your knife, scrape the garlic into the center of the board and repeat—chopping and scraping the garlic across the board with your knife—until you have a pastelike texture.

3. Place the garlic paste in a small bowl. Add the thyme, pepper, and olive oil and mix together to make a paste. Rub the roast with the garlic-thyme paste and massage it into the meat. Season liberally with salt.

4. Place the roast on an elevated rack in a roasting pan, insert a leave-in meat thermometer (if you have one), and place in the oven.

5. Roast for 30 minutes, then reduce the temperature to 350°F (175°C). Continue cooking until the roast reaches the desired doneness: 125°F (52°C) for medium-rare; 130°F (55°C) for medium; or 135°F (57°C) for medium-well, the latter being criminal, of course. Let rest for 20 minutes, then carve and serve.

Mongolian Beef
over Cauliflower Rice

serves: **3 to 4** | prep time: **15 minutes** | cook time: **15 minutes**

Ingredients

3 to 4 cups (540 to 720 grams) Cauliflower Rice (page 235)

2 tablespoons coconut oil

½ medium yellow onion, diced

½ cup (120 ml) coconut aminos

¼ cup (60 ml) organic honey

2 cloves garlic, minced

½ teaspoon grated fresh ginger

½ teaspoon red pepper flakes

pinch of coarse sea salt and freshly ground black pepper

2 tablespoons arrowroot powder

1 pound (455 grams) flank steak, thinly sliced against the grain

3 to 4 fried eggs (optional)

1 green onion, sliced, for garnish

Process

1. Make the cauliflower rice.

2. While the rice cooks, make the Mongolian beef: Heat the coconut oil in a large pan over medium heat. Add the onion and cook for 2 minutes, then add the coconut aminos, honey, garlic, ginger, red pepper flakes, and a pinch of salt and pepper.

3. Let the mixture come to a low boil. Then add the arrowroot powder to the pan, 1 tablespoon at a time, while continuously whisking until the mixture is thickened, about 5 minutes.

4. Place the steak slices in the pan with the sauce, distributing them throughout the pan so as not to overcrowd them. Simmer the meat in the sauce for 8 to 10 minutes, or until no red meat is apparent, flipping halfway through.

5. Once the meat has cooked through, place over cauliflower rice and top with a fried egg, if desired, and the chopped green onion.

The Perfect Burger

serves: **3** | prep time: **10 minutes** | cook time: **12 minutes**

Ingredients

For the burgers

1 pound (455 grams) ground beef

¼ medium red onion, minced

1 tablespoon Dijon mustard

1 teaspoon granulated garlic

½ teaspoon coarse sea salt

½ teaspoon freshly ground black pepper

For the shoestring parsnip fries

2 medium parsnips, peeled

½ cup (100 grams) coconut oil, melted

Garnishes

romaine hearts, leaves separated

sliced red onions

¾ cup (180 ml) Avocado Mousse (page 297)

shoestring parsnip fries (from above)

Process

1. In a medium mixing bowl, mix together all the ingredients for the burgers without overworking the meat.

2. Divide the meat into 3 equal portions and form into patties ½ inch (12 mm) thick. Use your thumb to make an indentation in the center of each burger. Set aside.

3. Using a spiral slicer or julienne slicer, cut the parsnips into strings.

4. Preheat the grill to medium high heat, and preheat a medium saucepan over medium-high heat. Once the grill is hot, place the burgers on the grill grate and close the lid. Cook for 6 minutes, then flip the burgers and cook for 2 to 3 minutes for medium-rare, or to the desired doneness.

5. While the burgers are cooking, add the coconut oil to the hot saucepan. Test the oil by placing a parsnip shoestring in the oil: if the oil bubbles furiously, it's ready. Fry the parsnips in the oil for 1 to 2 minutes, until golden brown. Place the fried parsnips on a paper towel–lined plate to drain.

6. When the burgers are done, remove them from the grill and let rest for 5 to 7 minutes.

7. To assemble the burgers, place each patty on a bed of lettuce and top with sliced red onions, ¼ cup (60 ml) of the avocado mousse, and parsnip fries.

Rosemary Sun-Dried Tomato Meatballs with Tomato Sauce

serves: **4** | prep time: **10 minutes** | cook time: **8 hours**

Ingredients

For the meatballs

2 pounds (910 grams) ground beef

1 packed cup (85 grams) sun-dried tomatoes, minced

1 medium red onion, minced

4 cloves garlic, minced

2 tablespoons minced fresh rosemary (1 sprig)

1 jalapeño pepper, minced (leave the seeds in if you want more heat)

2 large eggs

1 tablespoon chopped fresh Italian parsley

2 teaspoons coarse sea salt

2 teaspoons freshly ground black pepper

1 (24-ounce/680-g) jar of your favorite tomato sauce

Process

1. Place all the ingredients for the meatballs in a large mixing bowl. Without overworking the meat, gently combine the ingredients so they are evenly distributed. Then use your hands to form 8 large meatballs.

2. Line the bottom of a slow cooker with the meatballs. Pour the tomato sauce over the meatballs, cover, and cook on low for 8 hours.

note:

For faster cooking, place the meatballs in a baking dish, cover with the sauce, and bake uncovered in a 400°F (205°C) oven for 20 to 25 minutes, or until the meatballs are cooked through.

Chicken Dishes

Chicken Apricot Curry

serves: **6** | prep time: **10 minutes** | cook time: **20 minutes**

Ingredients

1 tablespoon coconut oil

3 cloves garlic, minced

2 (14-ounce/415-ml) cans full-fat coconut milk

1 teaspoon grated fresh ginger

2 tablespoons curry powder

1 tablespoon ground cumin

2 teaspoons ground coriander

1 teaspoon red pepper flakes

½ teaspoon ground cinnamon

½ teaspoon garam masala

pinch of coarse sea salt

pinch of freshly ground black pepper

1 large head cauliflower (about 2¼ pounds/1 kg), cut into small florets

1 red onion, diced

1½ pounds (680 grams) skinless, boneless chicken breast, cubed

1 cup (120 grams) dried apricots, roughly chopped

leaves from 1 or 2 sprigs fresh cilantro, for garnish

Process

1. Heat the coconut oil in a Dutch oven or medium stockpot over medium heat. Add the garlic and sauté just until fragrant, about 5 minutes.

2. Add the coconut milk, ginger, spices, salt, and pepper. Let simmer for 3 minutes.

3. Add the cauliflower and red onion. Cover and let simmer for 5 minutes.

4. Add the cubed chicken and apricots. Cover and let simmer on low for no more than 10 minutes, or until the cauliflower is fork-tender and the chicken is cooked through. Top each serving with cilantro leaves.

Honey Mustard Chicken Thighs

serves: **4** | prep time: **5 minutes** | cook time: **35 minutes**

Ingredients

juice of 2 lemons

¼ cup (60 ml) extra virgin olive oil

1 teaspoon garlic powder

2 pounds (910 grams) bone-in, skin-on chicken thighs

pinch of coarse sea salt and freshly ground black pepper

1 clove garlic, minced

1 teaspoon fresh thyme leaves, minced

1 teaspoon Dijon mustard

2 tablespoons raw organic honey, melted

Process

1. Preheat the oven to 400°F (205°C).

2. Combine the lemon juice, olive oil, and garlic powder in a mixing bowl and mix well. Add the chicken thighs and stir to coat the chicken in the mixture.

3. Place the chicken thighs on an elevated rack on a rimmed baking sheet. Season each chicken thigh with a pinch of salt and pepper. Place in the oven and roast for 30 minutes.

4. While the chicken is roasting, combine the garlic, thyme, mustard, and honey in a small bowl and mix well. At the 30-minute mark, brush the chicken thighs with the honey mustard and bake for an additional 5 minutes. Remove from the oven and serve. Garnish with extra honey mustard.

Lemon & Chive Pasta with Chicken Thighs

serves: **2** | prep time: **30 minutes** | cook time: **50 minutes**

Ingredients

2 bone-in, skin-on chicken thighs (about 10 ounces/280 grams)

pinch of coarse sea salt and freshly ground black pepper

3 large zucchini (about 1⅓ pounds/600 grams)

½ cup (120 ml) Lemon Chive Mayo (page 290)

1 tablespoon coconut oil

Process

1. Preheat the oven to 400°F (205°C).

2. Place the chicken thighs on an elevated rack on a rimmed baking sheet. Season each chicken thigh with a pinch of salt and pepper. Place in the oven and roast for 35 to 40 minutes, or until done (no pink should be visible).

3. While the chicken is cooking, peel the zucchini and then use a spiral slicer to cut them into noodles (see Note). Line a baking sheet with a couple of layers of paper towels. Spread the zucchini noodles across the paper towels, sprinkle liberally with salt to draw out the liquid, and place additional paper towels on top to absorb the liquid. Let the noodles rest for 30 minutes before cooking. Change the top layer of paper towels once to ensure all the liquid is soaked up.

4. While the zucchini is resting, make the mayo. Scoop out ½ cup (120 ml) of the mayo for this recipe; place the remaining mayo in the fridge for another use (it will keep for 1 week).

5. Heat the coconut oil in a pan over medium heat. Add the zucchini noodles with a pinch of salt and cook for 4 to 5 minutes, until the noodles become soft. Remove the pan from the heat. Pour the mayo into the pan and mix well to combine with the noodles.

6. Divide the noodles between 2 plates and top each portion with a cooked chicken thigh.

note:

No spiral slicer? Thinly slice the zucchini into fettuccine-like noodles, or use a julienne slicer to cut the zucchini.

Lemon Rosemary Roasted Chicken

serves: **4** | prep time: **10 minutes** | cook time: **1 hour 15 minutes**

Ingredients

1 (5-pound/2.25-kg) chicken, giblets removed

coarse sea salt and freshly ground black pepper

¼ cup (50 grams) lard, melted (coconut oil, bacon fat, duck fat all work)

1 lemon, cut in half

6 sprigs fresh rosemary

½ medium white onion, sliced

Process

1. Preheat the oven to 450°F (230°C) and set a rack in the middle position.

2. Rinse the chicken under cold running water and pat dry. Liberally season the inside of chicken with salt and pepper. Generously rub the lard on the outside of the chicken. Season the outside of the chicken with salt and pepper.

3. Place the lemon halves and 2 of the rosemary sprigs inside the cavity of the chicken. Line the bottom of a 12-inch (30.5-cm) cast-iron skillet with the onion slices. Place the remaining 4 sprigs of rosemary in the center of the skillet on top of the onion slices. Place the chicken on top of the rosemary, breast side down.

4. Place the pan in the oven and roast for 30 minutes, then reduce the heat to 350°F (175°C) and cook for another 60 to 90 minutes, or until the juices run clear when cut between the thigh and leg and the temperature in the breast reaches 160°F (70°C). Remove from the oven, let rest for 15 minutes, then slice and serve.

Hot
Wings

serves: **4** | prep time: **5 minutes** | cook time: **30 minutes**

Ingredients

coconut oil, for greasing the wire rack

2 pounds (910 grams) chicken wings and/or drumsticks

1 teaspoon coarse sea salt

1 teaspoon freshly ground black pepper

1 teaspoon granulated garlic

1 cup (240 ml) Frank's Red Hot Sauce or your favorite hot sauce, plus extra for the table

Process

1. Preheat the oven to 425°F (218°C). Line a rimmed baking sheet with aluminum foil, place a wire rack on top, and grease the wire rack with coconut oil.

2. Arrange the chicken wings evenly on the wire rack and season with the salt, pepper, and granulated garlic. Place in the oven and roast for 15 minutes.

3. After 15 minutes, remove the wings from the oven and place in a large mixing bowl. Pour the hot sauce over the wings and toss until they are evenly coated.

4. Place the wings back on the wire rack and return to the oven for 15 more minutes. Remove the wings from the oven and serve. Toss them in more sauce if you like extra-spicy wings, or serve with extra hot sauce on the table.

Honey Ginger Wings

serves: **4** | prep time: **5 minutes** | cook time: **30 minutes**

Ingredients

coconut oil, for greasing the wire rack

2 pounds (910 grams) chicken wings and/or drumsticks

1 teaspoon coarse sea salt

1 teaspoon freshly ground black pepper

1 teaspoon granulated garlic

2 tablespoons coconut aminos

¼ cup (60 ml) organic honey, melted

1 tablespoon coconut oil, melted

1 teaspoon sesame oil

1 tablespoon freshly grated ginger

2 tablespoons sesame seeds

1 green onion, green part only, sliced

Process

1. Preheat the oven to 425°F (218°C). Line a baking sheet with aluminum foil, place a wire rack on top, and grease the wire rack with coconut oil.

2. Arrange the chicken wings evenly on the wire rack and season with the salt, pepper, and granulated garlic. Place in the oven and roast for 15 minutes.

3. While the wings are roasting, combine the coconut aminos, honey, melted coconut oil, sesame oil, and ginger in a large mixing bowl and whisk well.

4. Remove the wings from the oven and place them in the bowl with the honey and ginger mixture. (You may have to do this in batches depending on the size of the bowl.) Toss and coat all the wings, then place them back on the wire rack. Sprinkle the sesame seeds over the wings and return to the oven to roast for an additional 15 minutes.

5. Remove the wings from the oven, place in a bowl or on a plate, and garnish with the green onion slices.

Slow Cooker
Tomatillo Chicken

serves: **6** | prep time: **10 minutes** | cook time: **8 hours**

Ingredients

1½ pounds (680 grams) tomatillos

1 medium red onion, sliced

2½ pounds (1.2 kg) boneless, skinless chicken breasts

4 cloves garlic, minced

1 jalapeño pepper, minced (seed if desired for less heat)

1½ cups (360 ml) chicken broth

1 teaspoon coarse salt

½ teaspoon freshly ground black pepper

1 large handful cilantro, chopped, for garnish

Process

1. Remove and discard the husks from the tomatillos, wash the tomatillos, and cut them in half.

2. Line the bottom of a slow cooker with the red onion slices. Place the chicken breasts on top and then add the tomatillos, garlic, jalapeño, chicken broth, salt, and pepper.

3. Cook on low for 8 hours. Remove the chicken and shred in a bowl. Use an immersion blender to blend the contents of the slow cooker into a sauce.

4. Place the shredded chicken on a plate and pour the sauce on top of the chicken. Serve with chopped cilantro on top.

Spaghetti Squash
Chicken Fritters

makes: **8 fritters** | prep time: **30 minutes** | cook time: **20 minutes**

Ingredients

1 small spaghetti squash (about 2 pounds/910 grams)

2 cups (200 grams) finely chopped, leftover Lemon Rosemary Roasted Chicken (page 193)

½ cup (60 grams) finely chopped yellow onion

1 cup (100 grams) blanched almond flour

2 large eggs

½ teaspoon garlic powder

pinch of coarse sea salt

pinch of freshly ground black pepper

2 to 3 tablespoons bacon fat or coconut oil

Process

1. Preheat the oven to 400°F (205°C).

2. Cut the spaghetti squash in half lengthwise and place it cut side down on a rimmed baking sheet. Bake for 25 to 30 minutes, or until soft to the touch. Remove from the oven and let rest until cool enough to handle, then use a spoon to scoop out and discard the seeds. Use a fork to remove the spaghetti squash strands. Measure out 2 cups (280 grams) of the strands and place them in a large bowl.

3. To the squash, add the chicken, onion, almond flour, eggs, garlic powder, salt, and pepper. Mix well and form 8 patties, similar in shape to burger patties.

4. Heat 1 tablespoon of the bacon fat in a large sauté pan over medium heat. Add 2 to 3 patties to the pan and cook on both sides for a total of 4 to 5 minutes. Do not crowd the pan. Repeat with the rest of the patties, adding more oil to the pan as needed, until all the patties have been cooked.

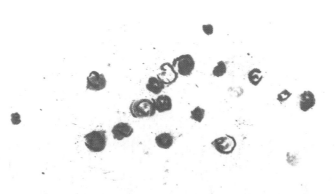

Fish & Seafood Dishes

Herb Cauliflower Mash with Seared Sea Scallops

serves: **2** | prep time: **10 minutes** | cook time: **5 minutes**

Ingredients

½ head cauliflower (12 ounces/340 grams), cut into florets

2 tablespoons full-fat coconut milk

1 teaspoon finely chopped fresh tarragon leaves, plus extra for garnish (optional)

1 teaspoon finely chopped fresh thyme leaves, plus extra for garnish (optional)

¼ teaspoon garlic powder

coarse sea salt and freshly ground black pepper, to taste

3 tablespoons coconut oil

8 sea scallops (about 6 ounces/160 grams)

Process

1. Steam the cauliflower florets and drain. Add the cauliflower to a food processor or blender and process until finely chopped. Add the coconut milk, scrape down the sides, and puree until smooth. Then add the tarragon, thyme, garlic powder, and salt and pepper and pulse just to combine. Set aside.

2. Heat the coconut oil in a large sauté pan over medium-high heat. Once the oil is hot, add the sea scallops, being sure not to crowd the pan. Sprinkle the scallops with salt and cook for about 90 seconds per side.

3. Place the scallops on top of the mashed cauliflower and serve. Garnish with some fresh thyme leaves and chopped tarragon leaves, if desired.

Creamy Seafood Risotto

serves: **4** | prep time: **30 minutes** | cook time: **15 minutes**

Ingredients

1 delicata or acorn squash (about 9 ounces/255 grams), cut in half lengthwise

3 cups (540 grams) Cauliflower Rice (page 235)

1 (14-ounce/415-ml) can full-fat coconut milk

½ teaspoon garlic powder

½ teaspoon onion powder

½ teaspoon white pepper

½ teaspoon coarse sea salt

½ teaspoon freshly ground black pepper

1 teaspoon red pepper flakes

2 tablespoons coconut oil

½ pound (225 grams) large shrimp, peeled and deveined

½ pound (225 grams) sea scallops

Process

1. Preheat the oven to 400°F (205°C).

2. Cut the delicata squash in half lengthwise. Place cut side down on a rimmed baking sheet. Bake for 30 minutes. Once soft, use a spoon to remove the seeds.

3. While the squash is cooking, make the cauliflower rice. (Leave the rice in the pan when it's finished cooking.)

4. In a large saucepan over medium heat, combine the coconut milk, garlic and onion powders, white pepper, salt, black pepper, and red pepper flakes. Use a spoon to scrape out the flesh from the squash and add it to the pan. Using a spatula, break up the squash until it becomes smooth and is fully incorporated into the coconut milk. Pour the thickened sauce into the saucepan with the cauliflower rice. Mix well.

5. Heat the coconut oil in a large saucepan over medium heat. Once the oil is hot, add the shrimp and scallops. Sprinkle with a small pinch of salt and cook for no more than 2 minutes per side, or until the shrimp and scallops are golden-brown on both sides.

6. Place the shrimp and scallops on top of the creamy risotto and serve.

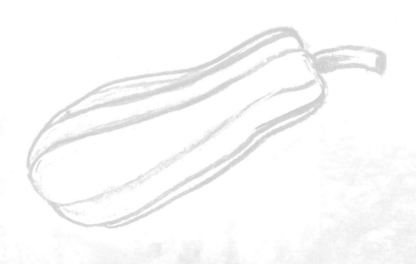

Shrimp Scampi

serves: **4** | prep time: **30 minutes** | cook time: **10 minutes**

Ingredients

1 small spaghetti squash (about 2 pounds/910 grams)

2 tablespoons coconut oil

½ small red onion, minced

3 cloves garlic, thinly sliced

1 teaspoon red pepper flakes

1 pound (455 grams) large shrimp with tails on, shelled and deveined (see Note)

½ cup (120 ml) vegetable broth

2 tablespoons finely chopped fresh Italian parsley

juice of 1 lemon

coarse sea salt and freshly ground black pepper, to taste

Process

1. Preheat the oven to 400°F (205°C). Line a rimmed baking sheet with parchment paper.

2. Cut the spaghetti squash in half lengthwise. Place cut side down on the prepared baking sheet. Cook for 25 to 30 minutes, or until soft to the touch. Remove from the oven and let rest until cool enough to handle, then use a spoon to scoop out and discard the seeds. Use a fork to remove the spaghetti squash strands. Set aside.

3. Heat the coconut oil in a large sauté pan over a medium-high heat. Add the red onion and sauté for 2 to 3 minutes, stirring often. Add the garlic and red pepper flakes and sauté for about a minute, until the garlic begins to brown.

4. Add the shrimp to the pan and cook for 1 minute. Add the vegetable broth and stir well to moisten the shrimp and spread them out evenly in the pan.

5. Cook for 2 to 3 minutes, flip the shrimp over, and cook for another minute, until the broth has cooked off.

6. Add the spaghetti squash threads and stir well for 1 to 2 minutes. Remove from the heat and add the parsley, lemon juice, and salt and pepper and stir well. Serve immediately.

note:

The shrimp can be prepared with the shell on or off. Shell-on preserves more flavor but is messier to eat. Shell-off makes eating a breeze.

Honey-Glazed Salmon with Pomegranate & Pineapple Salsa

serves: **4** | prep time: **10 minutes** | cook time: **5 to 8 minutes**

Ingredients

For the salsa

1 cup (150 grams) pomegranate seeds

1 cup (160 grams) diced pineapple

¼ cup (30 grams) diced red onion

1 tablespoon finely chopped jalapeño pepper

juice of 1 lime

pinch of coarse sea salt

4 (4-ounce/115-gram) pieces salmon, with skin

3 tablespoons coconut oil, melted

3 tablespoons organic honey, melted

⅛ teaspoon coarse sea salt

Process

1. In a medium bowl, mix together the ingredients for the salsa. Place in the refrigerator to keep cool.

2. Preheat the broiler to low and place an oven rack in the top position.

3. Place the salmon, skin side down, on a rimmed baking sheet. In a small bowl, whisk together the coconut oil and honey. Use a pastry brush to brush the mixture on the salmon, using it all. Sprinkle the salmon with the salt.

4. Broil for 5 to 8 minutes, until the salmon has begun to brown and is slightly flaky. Top the salmon with the salsa and serve.

Bacon-Wrapped Scallop
& Melon Skewers

makes: **4 skewers** | prep time: **10 minutes** | cook time: **25 minutes**

Ingredients

½ cantaloupe, honeydew, or
other melon of your choice
(about **10 ounces/280 grams**)

12 bay scallops (about **8
ounces/225 grams**)

3 slices bacon, cut crosswise
into **12 equal strips**

Process

1. Preheat the oven to 400°F (205°C). Line a rimmed baking sheet with
   parchment paper.

2. Use the large end of a melon baller to scoop out 12 melon balls.

3. Wrap a strip of bacon around each scallop, overlapping the ends. Place
   a bacon-wrapped scallop onto a metal or wooden skewer (see Note,
   page 173) through the overlapping ends to keep the bacon from falling
   off. Then add a melon ball. Repeat until you have 3 melon balls and 3
   scallops on each skewer.

4. Place the 4 skewers on the prepared baking sheet. Bake for 15
   minutes, then turn the skewers over and bake for another 10 minutes,
   or until the bacon is crisp and evenly cooked.

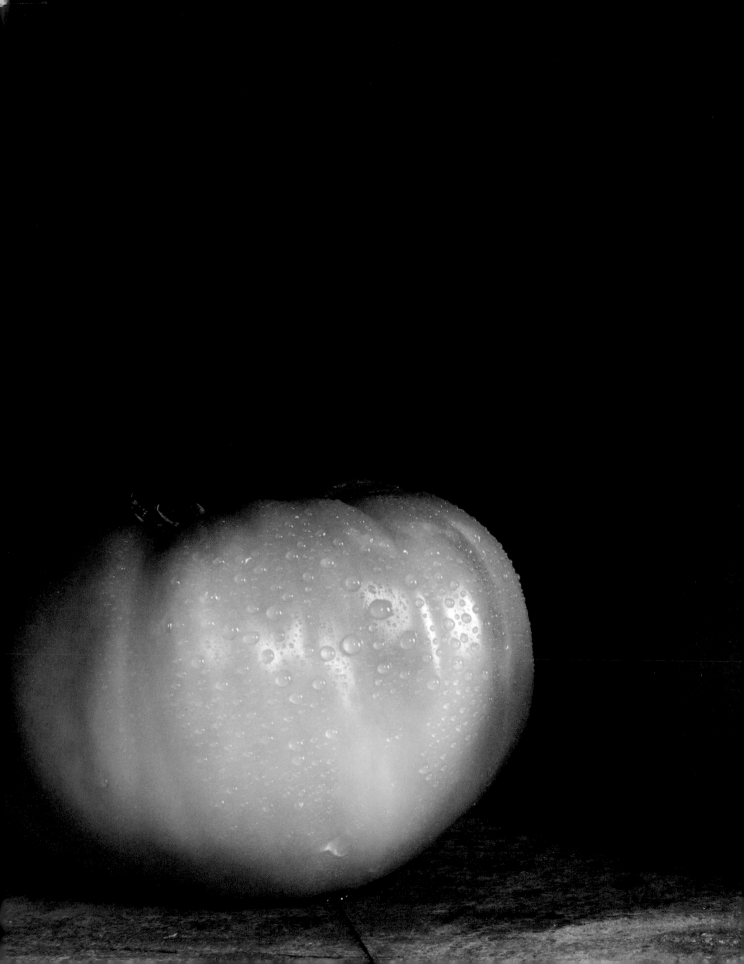

Honey Dijon & Rosemary Grilled Sweet Potatoes

serves: **4** | prep time: **10 minutes** | cook time: **45 minutes**

Ingredients

1 tablespoon finely chopped fresh rosemary, plus 3 rosemary sprigs

¼ cup (60 ml) Dijon mustard

⅓ cup (75 ml) organic honey

1 tablespoon olive oil

2 teaspoons coarse sea salt

2 teaspoons freshly ground black pepper

2 medium sweet potatoes or yams (about 1 pound/455 grams), thinly sliced, with skin

Process

1. Set up the grill for indirect heat and preheat it to medium.

2. In a large bowl, whisk together the finely chopped rosemary, mustard, honey, olive oil, salt, and pepper. Add the sweet potatoes to the bowl and toss to coat the sweet potatoes in the mixture. Your hands are the best tools for tossing and coating the potatoes.

3. Place 2 pieces of aluminum foil 18 inches (46 cm) long on top of each other, then dump out the sweet potatoes onto the foil. Spread the sweet potatoes out, leaving an inch of foil along the edges. Make sure the sweet potatoes don't overlap too much; if they do, they won't cook evenly. Place another 18-inch (46-cm) piece of aluminum foil on top, then fold the sides of the bottom piece of foil over the top and seal closed all around the edges.

4. Place the packet on the grill grate over indirect heat. Grill for 40 to 45 minutes with the lid closed, until you can easily pierce a sweet potato slice with a fork. They should be slightly browned. Taste a sweet potato and sprinkle with more salt and pepper if desired.

Dill Butternut
Squash Fries

serves: **4** | prep time: **15 minutes** | cook time: **35 minutes**

Ingredients

**1 large butternut squash (about
2 pounds/860 grams)**

**1 tablespoon coconut oil,
melted**

**3 tablespoons roughly chopped
fresh dill**

2 teaspoons coarse sea salt

Process

1. Preheat the oven to 400°F (205°C). Line a rimmed baking sheet with parchment paper.

2. Cut off the bottom of the butternut squash to create a stable surface. Holding the squash upright, use a sharp knife or peeler to remove the skin. Cut the squash in half lengthwise, remove the seeds, and cut it into fry-sized strips.

3. Toss the fries in a large bowl with the coconut oil, dill, and salt. Place the fries on the prepared baking sheet, making sure not to overlap them; if they overlap, they will steam rather than roast.

4. Bake for 35 minutes, or until tender on the inside and crunchy on the outside. Remove from the baking sheet and place on a cooling rack to help retain their crunch. Eat while still warm.

Bacon Lime Sweet Potato Salad

serves: **4** | prep time: **15 minutes** | cook time: **30 minutes**

Ingredients

½ pound (225 grams) bacon

3 large sweet potatoes (about 2 pounds/910 grams), cut into ½-inch (12-mm) cubes

4 cloves garlic, chopped

2 tablespoons coconut oil, melted

For the dressing

juice of 1 lime

2 tablespoons olive oil

2 tablespoons balsamic vinegar

2 green onions, sliced

1 handful of fresh dill, roughly chopped

dash of red pepper flakes

dash of ground cinnamon

fine-grain sea salt and freshly ground black pepper, to taste

Process

1. Preheat the oven to 375°F (190°C). Line a rimmed baking sheet with aluminum foil and lay the bacon flat on the sheet. Bake for 15 to 20 minutes, or until the bacon is slightly crispy. Let cool, then roughly chop and set aside. (Leave the oven on for the sweet potatoes.)

2. In a roasting pan or rimmed baking sheet lined with aluminum foil, toss the sweet potatoes and garlic in the coconut oil and roast for about 30 minutes, or until slightly browned.

3. While the sweet potatoes are roasting, make the dressing: Whisk together the lime juice, olive oil, and balsamic vinegar. Add the green onions, dill, red pepper flakes, cinnamon, and salt and pepper and mix well.

4. Once the sweet potatoes have finished cooking and are still warm, toss them with the dressing and chopped bacon.

Grilled
Baby Bok Choy

serves: **4** | prep time: **5 minutes** | cook time: **7 minutes**

Ingredients

4 baby bok choy (about ¾ pound/340 grams), cut in half lengthwise

coarse sea salt and freshly ground black pepper, to taste

2 tablespoons coconut oil, melted

1 teaspoon balsamic vinegar

⅛ teaspoon garlic powder

⅛ teaspoon paprika

Process

1. Preheat the grill to medium-high heat.

2. Season the bok choy with salt and pepper on both sides.

3. In a small bowl, combine the coconut oil, balsamic vinegar, garlic powder, and paprika and mix well. Place the bok choy on the grill and brush with the coconut oil mixture.

4. Grill for 3 to 4 minutes, or until the leaves start to get crispy and have grill marks on them.

5. Flip them over, brush them with the coconut oil mixture once more, and grill for an additional 2 to 3 minutes. Remove from the grill and serve.

Bacon Pecan Cabbage

serves: **4** | prep time: **10 minutes** | cook time: **15 minutes**

Ingredients

6 slices bacon, diced

2 cloves garlic, minced

½ small head red cabbage, thinly sliced

½ small head green cabbage, thinly sliced

½ teaspoon freshly ground black pepper

pinch of coarse sea salt

½ cup (60 grams) pecan halves

Process

1. In a large sauté pan over medium-high heat, cook the bacon until slightly crispy, then remove and set aside. Leave the rendered fat in the pan.

2. Return the pan with the bacon fat to medium heat and add the minced garlic and thinly sliced cabbage. Sprinkle with the pepper and salt, stir, and cook until softened and reduced, about 15 minutes. Be sure to stir it every few minutes so it cooks evenly.

3. When the cabbage is nearly done, toast the pecans in a small skillet over medium heat for 4 to 5 minutes, until they are slightly browned and aromatic.

4. Once the cabbage is done, add the pecans and cooked bacon to the pan with the cabbage and mix well before serving.

Asian Marinated Asparagus

serves: **5** | prep time: **1 to 4 hours** | cook time: **25 minutes**

Ingredients

¼ cup (50 grams) coconut oil, melted

2 tablespoons coconut aminos

1 tablespoon organic honey

½ teaspoon cayenne pepper

¼ teaspoon garlic powder

¼ teaspoon onion powder

1 pinch plus ¼ teaspoon coarse sea salt, divided

pinch of freshly ground black pepper

25 thin asparagus stalks (about 1 pound/455 grams), ends trimmed

5 slices bacon

2 teaspoons sesame seeds

Process

1. In a medium bowl, whisk together the coconut oil, coconut aminos, honey, cayenne pepper, garlic and onion powders, a pinch of the salt, and the pepper. Place the asparagus stalks and marinade in a large resealable bag and marinate in the refrigerator for at least 1 hour, but no more than 4 hours.

2. Preheat the oven to 400°F (205°C).

3. Bundle 5 asparagus stalks together, wrap them with a slice of bacon, and place them on a rimmed baking sheet. Repeat with the remaining asparagus and bacon. Sprinkle the bundles evenly with the sesame seeds and the remaining ¼ teaspoon of salt. Bake for 25 minutes. Serve warm.

Honey Lime
Roasted Carrots

serves: **2** | prep time: **10 minutes** | cook time: **55 minutes**

Ingredients

¼ cup (50 grams) coconut oil, melted

1 tablespoons organic honey, plus more for drizzling on top

juice of 1 lime

zest of 1 lime, divided

8 large carrots (about 1½ pounds/680 grams), thick or rough skin peeled

generous pinch of coarse sea salt

Process

1. Preheat the oven to 400°F (205°C).

2. Mix together the coconut oil, honey, lime juice, and half of the lime zest. Place the carrots in a glass baking dish and pour the lime juice mixture on top. Turn the carrots to evenly coat them in the juice mixture and sprinkle them with salt.

3. Bake for 50 to 55 minutes, or until the carrots are slightly brown and soft. Sprinkle with the rest of the lime zest and drizzle with a bit more honey.

Coconut Cauliflower Curry

serves: **2** | prep time: **15 minutes** | cook time: **25 minutes**

Ingredients

2 tablespoons coconut oil

2 cloves garlic, minced

1 medium red bell pepper, seeded and diced

1 large head cauliflower (about 2¼ pounds/1 kg), cut into florets

2 tablespoons curry powder

½ teaspoon red pepper flakes

¼ teaspoon ground cinnamon

⅛ teaspoon ground coriander

pinch of coarse sea salt and freshly ground black pepper

1 (14-ounce/415-ml) can full-fat coconut milk

2 tablespoons almond butter

sliced green onions, for garnish

Process

1. Place a medium saucepan over medium heat and add the coconut oil and garlic. Once the garlic is fragrant, add the bell pepper and cauliflower. Stir the vegetables to evenly coat them in the garlic and oil.

2. Add the curry powder, red pepper flakes, cinnamon, coriander, and salt and pepper. Stir to evenly coat the cauliflower in the spices, then add the coconut milk and almond butter. Mix to incorporate.

3. Cover the pan and cook for 20 to 25 minutes, or until the cauliflower is softened. Taste for seasoning and add more salt if needed. Garnish with the sliced green onions.

Parsnip Puree

makes: **3 cups (540 grams)** | prep time: **10 minutes** | cook time: **25 minutes**

Ingredients

2 pounds (910 grams) parsnips, peeled

2 tablespoons coconut oil, melted

¼ cup (60 ml) full-fat coconut milk

1 cup (240 ml) water

1 teaspoon dried thyme

½ teaspoon ground cinnamon

½ teaspoon coarse sea salt

⅛ teaspoon freshly grated nutmeg

pinch of freshly ground black pepper

½ teaspoon fresh thyme leaves, for garnish (optional)

Process

1. Preheat the oven to 400°F (205°C). Line a rimmed baking sheet with parchment paper.

2. Trim the ends of the parsnips, cut them in half crosswise, then cut the thick halves lengthwise into quarters. This will expose the inner core, which can be stringy. Holding each parsnip quarter upright on the cutting board, cut out the inner core with a paring knife and discard.

3. Place the parsnips in a medium mixing bowl. Add the coconut oil, toss well to coat, and place on the prepared baking sheet. Roast in the oven for 20 to 25 minutes, turning halfway through, until the parsnips are golden brown.

4. Place the parsnips in a blender or food processor and add the coconut milk and water. Blend until pureed, then add the thyme, cinnamon, salt, and nutmeg and blend again. If you would like the puree to be thinner, you can add ¼ cup (60 ml) water at a time until you get the consistency you desire.

5. Spoon into a bowl and sprinkle on the pepper and, if desired, the thyme leaves.

Cauliflower Rice

makes: 4 to 5 cups (720 to 900 grams) | prep time: 5 minutes | cook time: 10 to 13 minutes

Ingredients

1 large head (about 2¼ pounds/
1 kg) cauliflower, cut into florets

2 tablespoons coconut oil

⅓ cup (75 ml) broth (vegetable,
chicken, or beef)

coarse sea salt and freshly
ground black pepper, to taste

Process

1. Using the shredding attachment on a food processor, shred the cauliflower florets into rice-sized pieces.

2. Heat the coconut oil in a medium saucepan over medium heat. Add the cauliflower rice to the pan and cook for about 10 seconds, stirring, then add the broth and stir to combine. Cover and cook for 5 to 8 minutes. Sprinkle with salt and pepper, mix well, and cook, uncovered, for 5 more minutes, stirring every minute or so to keep the rice from sticking to the pan.

Refreshing Smoothies & Warming Drinks

Watermelon Mint Chiller

makes: **4 (2-cup/480-ml) servings** | prep time: **10 minutes**

Ingredients

10 cups (1.4 kg) diced seedless watermelon, chilled

juice of 2 limes

10 fresh mint leaves

balsamic vinegar, for garnish

Process

1. In a blender, puree the diced watermelon with the lime juice.

2. Set a fine-mesh strainer over a large bowl and strain the watermelon puree. Press lightly on the watermelon pulp to extract the juice without pushing the pulp through the strainer.

3. Rinse out the blender and return the strained watermelon to it. Blend in the mint leaves. Transfer to a punch bowl or pitcher.

4. Garnish with a few drops of balsamic vinegar and serve cold.

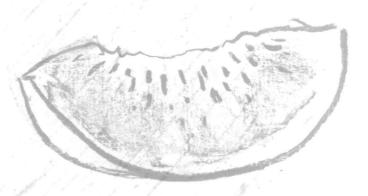

Afternoon Pick-Me-Up
(Coffee Smoothie)

makes: **4 (10-ounce/295-ml) servings** | prep time: **5 minutes**

Ingredients

1 medium banana

**1 cup (240 ml) brewed coffee,
chilled**

**1 cup (240 ml) almond milk
(page 313)**

**½ cup (120 grams) almond
butter**

¼ cup (60 ml) maple syrup

4 cups (455 grams) crushed ice

**unsweetened cocoa powder, for
garnish (optional)**

**shaved dark chocolate, for
garnish (optional)**

Process

Place all the ingredients except the ice in a blender and blend until smooth. Add the crushed ice and blend once more until thick. Garnish with a dusting of cocoa powder and shaved dark chocolate and serve immediately.

Hazelnut
Hot Chocolate

makes: **1 (1-cup/240-ml) serving** | prep time: **5 minutes** | cook time: **5 minutes**

Ingredients

1 cup (240 ml) hazelnut or other nut milk (page 313)

3 teaspoons unsweetened cocoa powder, plus extra for garnish

2 tablespoons Coconut Butter (page 305)

⅛ teaspoon vanilla extract

1 teaspoon organic honey

2 ounces (55 grams) Eating Evolved baking chocolate (72-percent cacao), chopped, or heaping ¼ cup (2 ounces/55 grams) Enjoy Life Mini Chocolate Chips

coconut milk whipped cream, for garnish (optional; see Note)

Process

Place the nut milk, cocoa powder, coconut butter, vanilla, and honey in a saucepan. Stir well to combine. Bring the mixture to a low boil, then remove from the heat. Add the chocolate and stir until the chocolate has melted. Garnish with a dusting of cocoa powder and, if desired, a dollop of whipped cream. Serve immediately.

note:

To make coconut milk whipped cream, first chill a 14-ounce can of coconut milk overnight. The next day, carefully scoop off the firm layer of coconut cream on top. (Reserve the coconut water for smoothies.) Place the cream in a mixing bowl or the bowl of a stand mixer with a whisking attachment. Add 1 tablespoon honey and whisk until the coconut cream forms stiff peaks.

Cinnamon
Pecan Latte

makes: **1 (12-ounce/360-ml) serving** | prep time: **5 minutes** | cook time: **5 minutes**

Ingredients

**½ cup (120 ml) pecan milk
(page 313)**

**1 cup (240 ml) freshly brewed
hot coffee**

1 tablespoon organic honey

1 teaspoon ground cinnamon

Process

Warm the pecan milk in a small saucepan over medium heat. Add the
rest of the ingredients and heat just to a bare simmer while stirring. Serve
immediately.

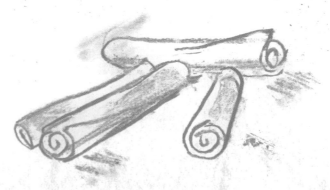

Gingerbread Latte

makes: **1 (12-ounce/360-ml) serving** | prep time: **5 minutes** | cook time: **5 minutes**

Ingredients

½ cup (120 ml) hazelnut or other nut milk (page 313)

1 cup (240 ml) freshly brewed hot coffee

2 tablespoons maple syrup

¼ teaspoon ground ginger

⅛ teaspoon ground cinnamon

⅛ teaspoon vanilla extract

Process

Warm the hazelnut milk in a small saucepan over medium heat. Add the rest of the ingredients and heat just to a bare simmer while stirring. Serve immediately.

Pineapple
Green Smoothie

makes: **3 (2-cup/480-ml) servings** | prep time: **5 minutes**

Ingredients

**2 cups (230 grams) chopped
fresh pineapple**

2 cups (50 grams) fresh spinach

**1 cup (20 grams) roughly
chopped fresh kale**

3 cups (720 ml) coconut water

¼ avocado

2 cups (300 grams) crushed ice

Process

Place all the ingredients except the ice in a blender and puree until
completely smooth. Add the ice and puree once more until the ice is
completely broken down and the texture is smooth.

Banana Berry Smoothie

makes: **2 (2-cup/480-ml) servings** | prep time: **5 minutes**

Ingredients

1 medium banana, peeled

2 cups (270 grams) frozen mixed berries

2 cups (480 ml) almond milk (page 313)

Process

Add all the ingredients to a blender and puree until completely smooth.

Ginger Apple Pear Smoothie

makes: **2 (2-cup/480-ml) servings** | prep time: **5 minutes**

Ingredients

1 teaspoon peeled and grated fresh ginger

1 large Honeycrisp apple, peeled, cored, and chopped

1 large pear, peeled, cored, and chopped

1 cup (240 ml) coconut water

2 cups (300 grams) crushed ice

Process

Place all the ingredients except the ice in a blender and puree until completely smooth. Add the ice and puree once more until the ice is completely broken down and the texture is smooth.

Orange Cream Smoothie

makes: **2 (2-cup/480-ml) servings** | prep time: **5 minutes**

Ingredients

2 oranges, peeled

**½ cup (120 ml) cashew milk
(page 313)**

½ teaspoon vanilla extract

zest of 1 orange

2 cups (300 grams) crushed ice

Process

Place all the ingredients except the ice in a blender and puree until completely smooth. Add the ice and puree once more until the ice is completely broken down and texture is smooth.

Desserts

Coffee Pecan Ice Cream

makes: **1 pint** | prep time: **2 hours to overnight** | cook time: **10 minutes**

Ingredients

1 (14-ounce/415-ml) can full-fat coconut milk

2 tablespoons strong brewed coffee

2 tablespoons organic honey

2 large egg yolks

1 teaspoon vanilla extract

½ cup (50 grams) chopped raw pecans

freshly ground coffee beans, for garnish (optional)

Process

1. Combine the coconut milk, coffee, honey, egg yolks, and vanilla in a saucepan. Heat gradually, whisking constantly, just until it comes to a low boil, then immediately remove the pan from the heat and let cool.

2. Transfer the mixture to a mixing bowl and cover with plastic wrap. Refrigerate for a minimum of 2 hours or overnight.

3. Place the cooled mixture in an ice cream maker and churn, following the manufacturer's directions, until the desired consistency is reached. Immediately scoop the ice cream out of the ice cream maker so it doesn't freeze to the sides of the bowl and stir in the chopped pecans by hand. Serve immediately, garnished with a sprinkle of ground coffee beans, or store, covered, in the freezer for up to 3 weeks.

note:

No ice cream maker? Once the mixture is tempered, transfer it to a bowl or bread pan and stick it in the freezer for 2 hours. Once frozen, just remove it from the freezer 15 minutes before serving to allow it to soften to a scoopable consistency. Scoop and serve.

Blueberry Rosemary Ice Cream

makes: **1 pint** | prep time: **2 hours to overnight** | cook time: **10 minutes**

Ingredients

1 (14-ounce/415-ml) can full-fat coconut milk

1 cup (150 grams) fresh blueberries

2 tablespoons organic honey

1 teaspoon minced fresh rosemary

1 teaspoon lemon extract

2 large egg yolks, whisked

Process

1. Combine the coconut milk, blueberries, honey, rosemary, and lemon extract in a blender or food processor. Blend until everything is well incorporated.

2. Pour the mixture into a saucepan over medium heat and add the egg yolks. Heat gradually, whisking constantly, just until it comes to a low boil, then immediately remove the pan from the heat and let cool. Transfer the mixture to a mixing bowl and cover with plastic wrap. Refrigerate for a minimum of 2 hours or overnight.

3. Place the cooled mixture in an ice cream maker and churn, following the manufacturer's directions, until the desired consistency is reached. Immediately scoop the ice cream out of the ice cream maker so it doesn't freeze to the sides of the bowl. Serve immediately or store, covered, in the freezer for up to 3 weeks.

note:

If you don't have an ice cream maker, once the mixture is chilled, transfer it to a bowl or bread pan and stick it in the freezer for 2 hours. Once frozen, just remove it from the freezer 15 minutes before serving to allow it to soften to a scoopable consistency. Scoop and serve.

Honey Pistachio
Ice Cream

makes: **1 pint** | prep time: **2 hours to overnight** | cook time: **10 minutes**

Ingredients

1 cup (120 grams) raw, shelled pistachios, plus ⅓ cup (40 grams) roughly chopped raw, shelled pistachios

1 (14-ounce/415-ml) can full-fat coconut milk

⅓ cup (75 ml) organic honey

1 teaspoon vanilla extract

pinch of coarse sea salt

Process

1. Place the whole pistachios in a food processor and pulse just until they reach a fine, flour-like consistency (do not continue to process beyond this point or the nuts will turn into a paste).

2. Combine the coconut milk, honey, vanilla, and salt in a saucepan over medium heat and whisk until everything is well incorporated. Whisk in the pistachio flour slowly. Once everything is well mixed, remove from the heat and let cool.

3. Transfer the mixture to a mixing bowl and cover with plastic wrap. Refrigerate for a minimum of 2 hours or overnight.

4. Place the cooled mixture in an ice cream maker and churn, following the manufacturer's directions, until the desired consistency is reached. When the ice cream is almost done, add the chopped pistachios while the ice cream maker is still on and continue running just until the pistachios are mixed throughout the ice cream.

5. Immediately scoop the ice cream out of the ice cream maker so it doesn't freeze to the sides of the bowl. Serve immediately or store, covered, in the freezer for up to 3 weeks.

note:

No ice cream maker? Once the coconut milk and pistachio flour mixture is chilled, mix in the chopped pistachios. Transfer to a bowl or bread pan and stick it in the freezer for 2 hours. Once frozen, just remove it from the freezer 15 minutes before serving to allow it to soften to a scoopable consistency. Scoop and serve.

Chocolate Cookie
Ice Cream

makes: **1 pint** | prep time: **2 hours to overnight** | cook time: **10 minutes**

Ingredients

1 (14-ounce/415-ml) can full-fat coconut milk

⅓ cup (75 ml) organic honey

1 teaspoon vanilla extract

⅛ teaspoon ground cinnamon

pinch of coarse sea salt

¼ cup (25 grams) unsweetened cocoa powder

3 Macadamia Chocolate Chip Cookies (page 267), frozen then roughly chopped

Process

1. Combine the coconut milk, honey, vanilla, cinnamon, and salt in a saucepan over medium heat and whisk until everything is well incorporated. Whisk in the cocoa powder. Once everything is well mixed, remove from the heat and let cool.

2. Transfer the mixture to a mixing bowl and cover with plastic wrap. Refrigerate for a minimum of 2 hours or overnight.

3. Once the mixture is cool, pour it into an ice cream maker and churn, following the manufacturer's directions, until the desired consistency is reached. When the ice cream is almost done, add the chopped cookies while the ice cream maker is still on and continue running just until the cookies are mixed throughout the ice cream.

4. Immediately scoop the ice cream out of the ice cream maker so it doesn't freeze to the sides of the bowl. Serve immediately or store, covered, in the freezer for up to 3 weeks.

Macadamia
Chocolate Chip
Cookies

Macadamia Chocolate Chip Cookies

makes: **20 cookies** | prep time: **20 minutes** | cook time: **13 to 15 minutes**

Ingredients

1 cup (220 grams) Macadamia Nut Butter (page 307), or store-bought

¼ cup (60 ml) organic honey

¼ cup (50 grams) coconut oil

1 teaspoon vanilla extract

1 large egg, whisked

2 tablespoons coconut flour

pinch of fine-grain sea salt

½ cup (3½ ounces/100 grams) Enjoy Life Mini Chocolate Chips

Process

1. Preheat the oven to 350°F (175°C). Line 2 baking sheets with parchment paper.

2. Combine the macadamia nut butter, honey, coconut oil, vanilla, and egg in a large bowl and mix well by hand using a wooden spoon or spatula. Add the coconut flour and salt and mix well, then fold in the chocolate chips. Refrigerate the batter until it has cooled and firmed up slightly, about 10 to 12 minutes.

3. Use a medium cookie scoop to drop balls of cookie dough onto the prepared baking sheets, 10 cookies per baking sheet. Bake for 13 to 15 minutes, or until the cookies are slightly browned. Remove from the oven and transfer to a rack immediately to cool.

Lemon Poppyseed Cookies

makes: **9 cookies** | prep time: **10 minutes** | cook time: **20 minutes**

Ingredients

1 cup (85 grams) blanched almond flour

1 tablespoon coconut flour, sifted

½ teaspoon baking soda

pinch of fine-grain sea salt

2 large eggs, whisked

¼ cup (60 ml) organic honey

2 tablespoons coconut oil, melted

1 teaspoon vanilla extract

juice of 2 lemons

zest of 1 lemon

1 teaspoon poppyseeds

Process

1. Preheat the oven to 350°F (175°C). Line a baking sheet with parchment paper.

2. Combine the almond flour, coconut flour, baking soda, and salt in a large bowl and whisk together. Add the eggs, honey, coconut oil, vanilla, lemon juice, and lemon zest and mix with a spatula until well combined. Fold in the poppyseeds.

3. Use a medium cookie scoop to drop 9 cookies onto the prepared baking sheet.

4. Bake for 20 minutes, or until the cookies have slightly browned. Remove from the oven and transfer to a rack immediately to cool.

No-Bake Tropical Escape Cookies

makes: **12 to 15 small cookies** | prep time: **2 hours**

Ingredients

2 dried pineapple rings (about 3½ ounces/100 grams), roughly chopped

2 dried papaya spears (about 1¾ ounces/50 grams), roughly chopped

2 dried mango pieces (about ¾ ounce/20 grams), roughly chopped

1 cup (95 grams) raw pecans

½ cup (35 grams) unsweetened shredded coconut

Process

1. Combine all the ingredients in a food processor. Pulse until the ingredients are well blended and slightly chunky.

2. Place 1 to 2 tablespoons of the mixture in each well of a mini muffin tin. Press down on the dough to firm up the cookies.

3. Place the tin in the refrigerator for at least 2 hours. Serve chilled. Store in a container in the refrigerator for up to 2 weeks.

Gingersnap Pumpkin Butter Cookie Sandwiches

makes: **20 cookie sandwiches** | prep time: **10 minutes** | cook time: **10 minutes**

Ingredients

For the cookies

2½ cups (250 grams) blanched almond flour, plus more for the work surface

¼ cup (30 grams) coconut flour, sifted

2 teaspoons baking powder

1½ tablespoons ground cinnamon

1 tablespoon ground ginger

pinch of fine-grain sea salt

¼ cup (50 grams) coconut oil, melted

4 tablespoons maple sugar

1 teaspoon vanilla extract

2 large eggs, whisked

For the pumpkin butter

2 cups (200 grams) raw pecans

2 tablespoons pumpkin puree

2 tablespoons maple syrup

½ cup (3½ ounces/100 grams) Enjoy Life Mini Chocolate Chips

coconut sugar, for garnish (optional)

Process

1. Preheat the oven to 350°F (175°C). Line a baking sheet with parchment paper.

2. In large mixing bowl, combine the almond flour, coconut flour, baking powder, cinnamon, ginger, and salt. Whisk together to evenly distribute the ingredients. Add the coconut oil, maple sugar, vanilla, and eggs and beat by hand or with an electric mixer until a dough has formed.

3. Dust the work surface with almond flour and lay the dough out, pressing down until it is about ½ inch (12 mm) thick.

4. Using a cookie cutter, cut the dough into 2½-inch (6-cm) circles. No cookie cutter? Use the lid to a spice jar or small mason jar. This should create around 40 small cookies.

5. Place 20 of the cookies on the prepared baking sheet about ½ inch (12 mm) apart and bake for 5 minutes. Immediately remove the cookies and place them on a rack to cool. Repeat with another batch of 20 or so cookies.

6. While the cookies cool, make the pumpkin butter. Place the pecans in a food processor and puree until smooth. Then add the pumpkin puree and maple syrup and puree until well combined.

7. Melt the chocolate in a double boiler over medium-low heat.

8. Assemble the sandwiches: Spread about 1 tablespoon of the pumpkin butter onto a cookie and top it off with another cookie. Use a spoon to drizzle a bit of melted chocolate over each cookie sandwich, then sprinkle with a pinch of coconut sugar. Store in an airtight container in the refrigerator for 3 to 4 days.

Candied Bacon
Chocolate Brownies

makes: **18 brownies** | prep time: **10 minutes** | cook time: **35 to 40 minutes**

Ingredients

coconut oil, for greasing the baking dish

2 cups (500 grams) almond butter

1 cup (240 ml) organic honey

2 large eggs, whisked

1 teaspoon vanilla extract

½ cup (50 grams) unsweetened cocoa powder

1 teaspoon baking soda

pinch of fine-grain sea salt

¾ cup (3½ ounces/100 grams) Enjoy Life Chocolate Chip Mega Chunks

5 strips Candied Bacon (page 113), roughly chopped, divided

large pinch of coconut sugar, for garnish

Process

1. Preheat the oven to 325°F (165°C). Grease a 13-by-9-inch (33-by-23-cm) baking dish with coconut oil.

2. In a large bowl, mix together the almond butter, honey, eggs, and vanilla. Mix in the cocoa powder, baking soda, and salt. Fold in the chocolate chunks, then fold in half of the candied bacon.

3. Pour the brownie mixture into the greased baking dish and smooth out the top. Sprinkle the top with the remaining candied bacon.

4. Bake for 35 to 40 minutes, or until a toothpick comes out clean when inserted in the middle. Let cool in the pan for about 5 minutes, then sprinkle with the coconut sugar. Cut into squares and serve.

Vanilla Bean Chocolate-Cayenne Cake

makes: **1 (8-inch/20-cm) single-layer cake** | prep time: **10 minutes** | cook time: **30 to 35 minutes**

Ingredients

coconut oil, for greasing the pan

1 cup (240 grams) coconut cream concentrate, softened

3 large eggs

½ cup (120 ml) organic honey

2 teaspoons vanilla extract

¼ cup (25 grams) unsweetened cocoa powder

1 teaspoon cayenne pepper

½ teaspoon baking soda

pinch of fine-grain sea salt

seeds from 2 vanilla beans (see Notes, page 87)

Process

1. Preheat the oven to 325°F (165°C). Grease an 8-by-8-inch (20-by-20-cm) cake pan with coconut oil.

2. Place all the ingredients in a large bowl and mix well. Pour the batter into the prepared cake pan, evening out the top with a spatula.

3. Bake for 30 to 35 minutes, or until a toothpick comes out clean when inserted in the middle of the cake. Remove from the oven and let cool in the pan on a cooling rack before cutting and serving.

Lime
Pound Cake

makes: **1 (9-inch/23-cm) single-layer cake** | prep time: **20 minutes** | cook time: **35 minutes**

Ingredients

For the cake

2 cups (185 grams) blanched almond flour

½ cup (65 grams) coconut flour, sifted

½ teaspoon fine-grain sea salt

1 teaspoon baking soda

⅔ cup (165 ml) coconut oil, melted, plus more for greasing the pan

⅔ cup (165 ml) organic honey, melted

4 large eggs

⅔ cup plus 3 tablespoons (165 ml) unsweetened full-fat coconut milk

2 tablespoons freshly squeezed lime juice

1 tablespoon finely grated lime zest

For the lime whipped cream

1 (14-ounce/415-ml) can full-fat coconut milk, chilled overnight

1 tablespoon organic honey

1 tablespoon freshly squeezed lime juice

1 teaspoon lime zest, cut into fine strips, for garnish

Process

1. Preheat the oven to 350°F (175°C). Lightly coat the interior of a 9-inch (23-cm) cake pan with coconut oil. Cut parchment paper to fit the bottom of the pan and place it over the coconut oil.

2. Sift the dry ingredients into a large mixing bowl and whisk to combine.

3. Place the oil and honey in the bowl of a food processor and process for 2 minutes. Add the eggs one at a time, processing after each addition. Add the coconut milk, lime juice, and lime zest, and continue to process until well combined.

4. Make a well in the center of the dry ingredients, then pour in the wet ingredients. Use a wooden spoon to thoroughly combine until smooth.

5. Pour the batter into the prepared pan and bake for 35 minutes, or until a toothpick inserted into the center of the cake comes out clean. Let the cake cool in the pan on a cooling rack for 10 minutes. Remove the cake from the pan and let it cool completely on a cooling rack.

6. While the cake is cooling, make the lime whipped cream: Open the chilled can of coconut milk and carefully scoop off the firm layer of coconut cream on the top, leaving the coconut water below it in the can. (Reserve the coconut water for making smoothies.) Place the cream in a mixing bowl or the bowl of a stand mixer with a whisking attachment. Add the honey and lime juice and whisk until the coconut cream forms stiff peaks.

7. When the cake is completely cool, top it with the lime whipped cream and garnish with the lime zest. Serve immediately or refrigerate until ready to serve. Store, covered, in the refrigerator for up to 5 days, or freeze for up to 3 months.

note:

Frost the cake once it is completely cool so the whipped coconut cream doesn't melt.

Frozen Blueberry Cheesecake

serves: **8 to 10** | prep time: **20 minutes,
plus 4 to 5 hours to freeze** | cook time: **20 minutes**

Ingredients

For the crust

⅔ **cup (80 grams) raw pecans**

1 cup (250 grams) almond butter

1 cup (70 grams) unsweetened shredded coconut

¼ **cup (80 grams) softened Coconut Butter (page 305)**

2 tablespoons organic honey

pinch of fine-grain sea salt

For the filling

2 cups (280 grams) raw cashews, soaked in water for 2+ hours and drained

½ **cup (120 ml) melted coconut oil**

½ **cup (120 ml) organic honey**

¼ **cup (60 ml) full-fat coconut milk**

3 tablespoons freshly squeezed lemon juice

1 teaspoon vanilla extract

For the topping

2 cups (300 grams) fresh blueberries, plus ½ **cup (75 grams) fresh blueberries for garnish**

⅓ **cup (75 ml) maple syrup**

Process

1. Make the crust: Place the pecans in a food processor and mix until they begin to form pecan butter. Add the almond butter, shredded coconut, coconut butter, honey, and salt and pulse until well combined.

2. Place the crust mixture in a springform pan, then press down and smooth it out so that the surface is even all around the pan. Put in the freezer to harden for 2 to 3 hours.

3. When the crust is hard, make the filling: Add the soaked cashews to a food processor and process until they fully break down into a chunky paste. Add the rest of the filling ingredients to the food processor and process until smooth (it should resemble a thin nut butter).

4. Pour the filling onto the hardened crust and smooth out the top. Place in the freezer and let settle and firm up for another 2 hours.

5. When filling has firmed up, make the topping: In a small saucepan over medium heat, combine 2 cups (300 grams) of blueberries and the maple syrup and cook for 15 minutes, or until most of the blueberries have burst. Reduce the heat to low and simmer until the mixture has thickened, about 5 minutes.

6. To serve, pour the warm blueberry topping on the top of the cheesecake and garnish individual slices with fresh blueberries. Serve immediately. Store leftovers in an airtight container in the freezer for up to 2 weeks.

note:

No springform pan? Use a pie pan or an 8-by-8-inch (20-by-20-cm) glass baking dish instead.

Black & White Cake

serves: **8** | prep time: **15 minutes** | cook time: **40 to 45 minutes**

This cake is flexible. It can be all chocolate or all vanilla, or you can use a combination of the two in a checkerboard pattern. For chocolate, just mix all the ingredients together; for vanilla, simply leave out the cocoa powder. To make a black and white cake, you will need a checkerboard cake pan.

Ingredients

For the cake

¾ cup (110 grams) coconut flour, sifted

1 teaspoon fine-grain sea salt

1 teaspoon baking soda

⅓ cup (30 grams) unsweetened cocoa powder, if making a black and white checkerboard cake; ½ cup (50 grams) unsweetened cocoa powder, if making a solid chocolate cake

10 large eggs

1 cup (200 grams) coconut oil, plus extra to grease the cake pan

1 cup (240 ml) maple syrup

For the ganache

1 cup (7 ounces/200 grams) Enjoy Life Mini Chocolate Chips

2 tablespoons lard (coconut oil works as well)

Process

1. Preheat the oven to 350°F (175°C). Grease a 9-inch (23-cm) cake pan with coconut oil and insert a round piece of parchment paper cut to the size of the bottom of the pan.

2. Make the cake: For a solid vanilla cake or black and white cake, whisk together the coconut flour, salt, and baking soda in a small bowl. For a solid chocolate cake, whisk together the coconut flour, salt, baking soda, and ½ cup (50 grams) cocoa powder in a small bowl.

3. In a large mixing bowl or stand mixer, combine the eggs, coconut oil, and maple syrup. Mix until well combined. Once the wet ingredients are blended, add the coconut flour mixture and blend until smooth.

4. If you are making a checkboard cake, pour half of the batter into a separate mixing bowl. Add ⅓ cup (30 grams) cocoa powder to the large mixing bowl and blend.

5. Pour the batter into the prepared pan. If you are making a checkerboard cake, place the batter dividing ring in the pan and pour the chocolate batter in the center and outer sections and the vanilla batter in the middle section.

6. Bake for 30 to 35 minutes, or until a toothpick inserted into the center of the cake comes out clean. Remove from the oven and let cool in the pan on a cooling rack.

7. When the cake is completely cool, make the ganache: Combine the chocolate chips and lard in a double boiler over medium heat and stir until melted and well combined, about 10 minutes.

8. Pour the ganache over the cake, letting it drip down the sides. Once the cake is covered, transfer it to the refrigerator and let the ganache solidify. Trim off the excess chocolate before plating. Slice and enjoy.

Chocolate Coffee Bread Pudding

serves: **4** | prep time: **10 minutes** | cook time: **25 to 30 minutes**

Ingredients

coconut oil, for greasing the ramekins

4 (1-inch/2.5-cm) slices leftover Cinnamon Chocolate Swirl Banana Bread (page 81)

2 large eggs

1 (14-ounce/415-ml) can full-fat coconut milk

3 tablespoons maple syrup

1 teaspoon vanilla extract

1 tablespoon coarsely ground coffee

⅛ teaspoon ground cinnamon

pinch of fine-grain sea salt

Process

1. Preheat the oven to 350°F (175°C). Grease 4 (3½-ounce/90-ml) ramekins with coconut oil.

2. Cut the leftover banana bread slices into crouton-sized pieces.

3. In a bowl, whisk together the eggs, coconut milk, maple syrup, vanilla, coffee, cinnamon, and salt.

4. Place the banana bread pieces in the ramekins, then pour the pudding mixture over the top. Put the ramekins on a rimmed baking sheet (to catch any spillovers) and place in the oven. Bake for 25 to 30 minutes, or until the top of bread pudding is golden brown. Let rest for 10 minutes before serving.

Individual Apple Crisps

serves: **4** | prep time: **20 minutes** | cook time: **15 minutes**

Ingredients

3 tablespoons unsalted grass-fed butter, softened, divided, plus extra for greasing the ramekins

2 medium apples, cored and thinly sliced

2 tablespoons ground cinnamon, divided

4 tablespoons coconut sugar, divided

2 pinches of fine-grain sea salt, divided

juice of 1 lemon

1 tablespoon maple syrup

1 tablespoon blanched almond flour

1 cup (95 grams) raw walnuts, roughly chopped

½ cup (65 grams) slivered almonds

Process

1. Preheat the oven to 350°F (175°C). Line a rimmed baking sheet with parchment paper. Grease 4 (3½-ounce/90-ml) ramekins with butter.

2. Melt 1 tablespoon of the butter in a large skillet over medium heat. Add the apples to the pan and stir to coat them in the butter. Cover the pan with a lid to help steam and soften the apples.

3. Once the apples are soft, about 10 minutes, sprinkle them with 1 tablespoon of the cinnamon, 2 tablespoons of the coconut sugar, a pinch of salt, and the lemon juice and mix well. Remove from the heat.

4. In a small bowl, mix together the maple syrup, almond flour, walnuts, and almonds along with the remaining 2 tablespoons of butter, 1 tablespoon of cinnamon, 2 tablespoons of coconut sugar, and pinch of salt.

5. Divide the cooked apples among the ramekins and top them with the nut mixture.

6. Place the ramekins on the prepared baking sheet (in case of spills) and bake for 15 minutes, or until the nut mixture has browned on top.

Condiments, Nut Butters, & Nut Milks

30-Second Mayo

makes: **1 cup (240 ml)** | prep time: **30 seconds**

Ingredients

1 large egg

¾ cup (180 ml) avocado oil

1 teaspoon freshly squeezed lemon juice

1 teaspoon Dijon mustard

pinch of fine-grain sea salt

To make any of the following flavored mayos, make the 30-Second Mayo and then fold in the additional ingredients.

Flavored Mayos

Maple Mayo

1 teaspoon maple syrup

Spicy Mayo

¼ to ½ cup (60 to 120 ml) hot sauce

Herb Mayo

1 tablespoon chopped fresh parsley leaves

1 tablespoon chopped fresh chives

1 tablespoon chopped fresh tarragon leaves

½ teaspoon minced garlic

Lemon Chive Mayo

3 tablespoons freshly squeezed lemon juice

1 tablespoon plus 1 teaspoon chopped fresh chives

Process

Place all the ingredients in a tall, narrow container (see Note). Place an immersion blender in the bottom of the container and turn it to high speed. The oil will begin to thicken. Once the bottom mixture thickens and turns off-white, begin to slowly lift the immersion blender upward to finish mixing the rest of the oil into the mayo. This mixing should take no more than 15 seconds. Store the mayo in an airtight container in the fridge. Use within 1 week.

note:

Finding the right container can take some improvising. You need one that's wide enough at the bottom to allow you to lower the immersion blender all the way down, but at the same time it needs to be narrow enough that when the ingredients are added to the container, they come up about 3 inches (7.5 cm). (If the container is too wide, the ingredients will spread out and won't cover the head of the immersion blender when it's inserted into the container.) We use a protein shaker bottle, which happens to have measurements on the side of the bottle, making measuring the avocado oil an easy, one-step process.

Crock-Pot Ketchup

makes: **2½ cups (600 ml)** | prep time: **10 minutes** | cook time: **8 hours**

Ingredients

1 medium yellow onion, diced

3 cloves garlic, minced

12 ounces (340 grams) tomato paste

½ cup water (120 ml)

¼ cup (60 ml) vegetable broth

½ cup (120 ml) organic honey, melted

¼ cup (60 ml) apple cider vinegar

1 teaspoon coarse sea salt

¼ teaspoon ground allspice

¼ teaspoon ground cloves

½ teaspoon mustard powder

1 teaspoon ground cinnamon

pinch of freshly ground black pepper

Process

1. Place the onion, garlic, tomato paste, water, vegetable broth, honey, and apple cider vinegar in a slow cooker. Use a spoon to stir the ingredients together. Add the salt, allspice, cloves, mustard powder, cinnamon, and pepper and stir again. Cover and cook on low for 8 hours.

2. Once the ketchup is done, remove the lid and use an immersion blender to blend the ketchup until smooth. (If you don't have an immersion blender, transfer the mixture in small batches to a blender to blend it.) Place the ketchup in mason jars or containers and let cool to room temperature before refrigerating. Store in the refrigerator for up to 4 weeks.

Pistachio Pesto

makes: **1 cup (240 ml)** | prep time: **5 minutes**

Ingredients

1 cup (125 grams) raw shelled pistachios

2 cloves garlic, roughly chopped

1 cup (25 grams) fresh basil leaves

½ to 1 cup (120 to 240 ml) extra virgin olive oil (see Note)

3 tablespoons freshly squeezed lemon juice

pinch of fine-grain sea salt and freshly ground black pepper

Process

Place the pistachios in a food processor and pulse until they are broken down into small pieces. Add the garlic and basil and turn the food processor on. While the food processor is running, slowly add the olive oil until the pesto is thickened to your liking. Add the lemon juice, salt, and pepper and pulse once more to combine. Store in an airtight container in the fridge. Use within 1 week.

note:

For a thick pesto, use only ½ cup (120 ml) extra virgin olive oil. For a thin pesto, use 1 cup (240 ml) extra virgin olive oil.

Garlic Aioli

makes: **1 cup (240 ml)** | prep time: **5 minutes**

Ingredients

1 large egg

1 scant cup (220 ml) avocado oil

1 teaspoon Dijon mustard

½ teaspoon freshly squeezed
lemon juice

3 cloves garlic, finely chopped

pinch of fine-grain sea salt and
freshly ground black pepper

Process

Place all the ingredients in a tall container. Place an immersion blender
in the bottom of the container and turn it to high speed. The mixture will
begin to thicken. As it thickens at the bottom, slowly pull the immersion
blender upward to thicken the mixture throughout. (This process should
take no more than 30 seconds.) Serve with Dill Butternut Squash Fries
(page 219).

Avocado Mousse

makes: **1 cup (240 ml)** | prep time: **15 minutes**

Ingredients

1 cup water (240 ml)

1 teaspoon fine-grain sea salt, plus more to taste

1 large avocado, peeled and pitted

juice of 1 lime

freshly ground black pepper, for garnish (optional)

Process

1. Combine the water and 1 teaspoon salt in a small bowl or container just large enough to hold the avocado. (A soak in salt water will slow the process of the avocado turning brown.)

2. Place the peeled and pitted avocado in the salt water. The avocado should be submerged in the salt water; if not, add a little more water and salt. Let it soak for 10 to 15 minutes. Remove from the water and place in a food processor. Add the lime juice and season with salt. Process until you have a smooth mousse. It can be piped with a pastry bag or by using a snipped corner of a resealable plastic bag. Serve with a sprinkling of pepper, if desired. Store in the refrigerator in a sealed container for up to 5 days.

Pico
de Gallo

makes: **2 cups (480 ml)** | prep time: **10 minutes**

Ingredients

**3 tomatoes (about ¾ pound/
340 grams), diced**

**¼ cup (30 grams) diced white
onion**

**½ jalapeño pepper, minced
(seed if desired for less heat)**

**1 handful of fresh cilantro, finely
chopped**

juice of 1 lime

Process

Mix all the ingredients together in a bowl. Let chill before serving. Store in an airtight container in the fridge and use within 1 week.

Blueberry BBQ Sauce

makes: **3 cups (720 ml)** | prep time: **10 minutes** | cook time: **40 to 55 minutes**

Ingredients

½ tablespoon bacon fat or coconut oil

½ medium sweet onion, diced

1½ tablespoons Dijon mustard

1 teaspoon apple cider vinegar

1 teaspoon ground cinnamon

¼ teaspoon coarse sea salt

juice of 1 lemon

1 cup (240 ml) chicken broth

¼ cup (60 ml) organic honey

1 (6-ounce/170-gram) jar or can tomato paste

12 ounces (340 grams) fresh or frozen blueberries, divided

Process

1. In a medium saucepan, heat the bacon fat over medium heat. Add the onion and sauté until soft and translucent, about 8 minutes, stirring often. Add the mustard, vinegar, cinnamon, and salt and sauté for 30 seconds.

2. Add the lemon juice, chicken broth, honey, and tomato paste and whisk together until smooth. Add half of the blueberries and remove the pan from the heat. Use an immersion blender to puree the sauce, or puree it in batches in a blender.

3. Put the sauce back over medium heat and stir in the remaining blueberries. Bring to a light boil, then reduce to a simmer and slightly cover with a lid. Simmer for 30 to 45 minutes to allow the flavors to meld. Let cool before using or bottling. Store in an airtight container in the refrigerator for up to a week, or freeze for up to 3 months.

Tangy
BBQ Sauce

makes: **2 cups (480 ml)** ǀ prep time: **10 mins** ǀ cook time: **40 to 50 mins**

Ingredients

½ tablespoon bacon fat or coconut oil

½ medium sweet onion, finely diced

3 cloves garlic, minced

1½ tablespoons Dijon mustard

1 tablespoon balsamic vinegar

1 teaspoon apple cider vinegar

1 teaspoon paprika

1 teaspoon chili powder

½ teaspoon ground cinnamon

¼ teaspoon coarse sea salt

juice of 1 lemon

1 cup (240 ml) low-sodium chicken broth

1 (6-ounce/170-gram) jar or can tomato paste

Process

1. In a saucepan, heat the bacon fat over medium heat. Add the onion and garlic and sauté, stirring often, until soft and translucent, about 8 minutes. Add the mustard, balsamic vinegar, apple cider vinegar, paprika, chili powder, cinnamon, and salt and sauté for 30 seconds.

2. Add the lemon juice, chicken broth, and tomato paste and whisk together until smooth. Bring to a light boil over medium heat, then reduce to a simmer and slightly cover with a lid. Simmer for 30 to 45 minutes to allow the flavors to meld. Let cool before using or bottling. Store in an airtight container in the refrigerator for up to a week, or freeze for up to 3 months.

Coconut Butter

makes: **1 cup (250 grams)** | prep time: **8 to 15 minutes**

Ingredients

**1½ cups (75 grams)
unsweetened coconut flakes**

Process

Place the coconut flakes in a food processor and process until the flakes break down into a smooth texture, stopping occasionally to scrape down the sides. This can take anywhere from 8 to 15 minutes. The longer it purees, the more it will develop a butter-like consistency. Store in the refrigerator in sealed container for up to 1 month. Coconut butter becomes hard when cold, but it can be softened or melted over heat in a small saucepan.

Macadamia
Nut Butter

makes: **2 cups (510 grams)** | prep time: **5 minutes**

Ingredients

**2 cups (265 grams) raw
macadamia nuts**

Process

Place the macadamia nuts in a food processor or high-speed blender and puree until smooth. Store in an airtight container in the refrigerator for up to 1 week.

Maple Cinnamon
Pecan Butter

makes: **1½ cups (380 grams)** | prep time: **5 minutes**

Ingredients

2 cups (210 grams) raw pecans

2 tablespoons maple syrup

1 teaspoon ground cinnamon

pinch of fine-grain sea salt

Process

Place the pecans, maple syrup, and cinnamon in a food processor or high-speed blender and puree until smooth. Store in an airtight container in the refrigerator for up to 1 week.

note:
For a creamier texture, add ¼ cup (60 ml) almond or walnut oil to the mixture before pureeing.

Vanilla Bean
Almond Butter

makes: **1½ cups (380 grams)** | prep time: **5 minutes**

Ingredients

2 cups (280 grams) raw almonds

1 tablespoon organic honey

1 teaspoon vanilla extract

seeds from 1 vanilla bean (see Notes, page 87)

pinch of fine-grain sea salt

Process

Place the almonds, honey, vanilla extract, vanilla bean seeds, and salt in a food processor or high-speed blender and puree until smooth. Store in an airtight container in the refrigerator for up to 1 week.

note:

for a creamier texture, add ¼ cup (60 ml) almond or walnut oil to the mixture before pureeing.

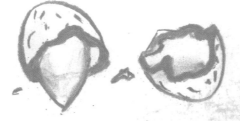

Homemade Nut Milks

makes: **3 to 4 cups (720 to 960 ml)** | prep time: **24 hours**

Ingredients

Almond Milk
1 cup (140 grams) raw almonds
3 cups (720 ml) filtered water

Cashew Milk
1 cup (140 grams) raw cashews
3 cups (720 ml) filtered water

Pecan Milk
1 cup (105 grams) raw pecans
3 cups (720 ml) filtered water

Walnut Milk
1 cup (105 grams) raw walnuts
3 cups (720 ml) filtered water

Hazelnut Milk
1 cup (145 grams) raw
hazelnuts, skins removed
3 cups (720 ml) filtered water

Process

1. To make any of these milks, place the nuts and filtered water in a jar. Close and let soak at room temperature for at least 24 hours.

2. Place the soaked nuts and water in a blender and blend for 1 to 2 minutes, until the nuts are very finely chopped. Using a nut milk strainer or a strainer lined with 5 or 6 layers of cheesecloth, strain the milk from the nuts. (Reserve the drained nuts for making nut meal; see Note.) Keep the milk in a closed jar in the refrigerator for up to 2 weeks. Shake well before using.

note:

To make nut meal with the drained nut pulp, spread the pulp on a parchment paper-lined rimmed baking sheet. Set the oven to 170°F (76°C), place the baking sheet in the oven with the door cracked open, and let dry for 3 hours. Let cool, then place in a food processor and chop to create the texture of a fine meal. Store in the refrigerator for up to a month.

Recommended Reading

SCIENTIFIC READS

Bailor, Jonathan. *The Calorie Myth: How to Eat More, Exercise Less, Lose Weight, and Live Better.* New York: HarperCollins Publishers, 2013. (Author's site: http://thesmarterscienceofslim.com)

Ballantyne, Sarah. *The Paleo Approach: Reverse Autoimmune Disease and Heal Your Body.* Las Vegas: Victory Belt Publishing, 2014. (Author's site: http://thepaleomom.com)

Kresser, Chris. *Your Personal Paleo Code: The 3-Step Plan to Lose Weight, Reverse Disease, and Stay Fit and Healthy for Life.* New York: Little, Brown and Company, 2013. (Author's site: http://chriskresser.com)

Minger, Denise. *Death by Food Pyramid: How Shoddy Science, Sketchy Politics, and Shady Special Interests Have Ruined Our Health.* Malibu: Primal Blueprint Publishing, 2014. (Author's site: http://rawfoodsos.com)

Sanfilippo, Diane. *Practical Paleo: A Customized Approach to Health and a Whole-Foods Lifestyle.* Las Vegas: Victory Belt Publishing, 2012. (Author's site: http://balancedbites.com)

Sisson, Mark. *The Primal Blueprint: Reprogram Your Genes for Effortless Weight Loss, Vibrant Health, and Boundless Energy.* Malibu: Primal Blueprint Publishing, 2013. (Author's site: http://marksdailyapple.com)

Wolf, Robb. *The Paleo Solution: The Original Human Diet.* Las Vegas: Victory Belt Publishing, 2010. (Author's site: http://robbwolf.com)

GEORGE ↘

Civilized Caveman Cooking Creations
civilizedcavemancooking.com

PaleOMG ← *JUII*
paleomg.com

Against All Grain
againstallgrain.com

Balanced Bites
balancedbites.com

BrittanyAngell
brittanyangell.com

Clean Eating with a Dirty Mind
cleaneatingwithadirtymind.com

The Clothes Make the Girl
theclothesmakethegirl.com

The Domestic Man
thedomesticman.com

Elana's Pantry
www.elanaspantry.com

Everyday Paleo
everydaypaleo.com

Fat-Burning Man
fatburningman.com

Health-Bent
health-bent.com

theKitchn
thekitchn.com

Nom Nom Paleo
nomnompaleo.com

Paleo Comfort Foods
paleocomfortfoods.com

Paleo Cupboard
paleocupboard.com

Paleo Parents
paleoparents.com

Primal Palate
primalpalate.com

Real Food Liz
realfoodliz.com

SlimPalate
slimpalate.com

The Spunky Coconut
thespunkycoconut.com

Stupid Easy Paleo
stupideasypaleo.com

Underground Wellness
undergroundwellness.com

The Urban Poser
urbanposer.blogspot.com

Whole9
whole9life.com

Zen Belly
zenbellycatering.com

RECIPE INDEX

Breakfast

Sun-Dried Tomato
Sweet Potato
Hash

Banana Bread
Waffles with Mixed
Fruit Topping

Pumpkin Waffles

Baked Banana
Chip Crusted
French Toast

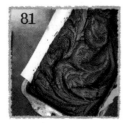

Cinnamon
Chocolate Swirl
Banana Bread

Sweet Potato
Quiche

Delicata Squash
Frittata

Lavender Vanilla
Bean Granola

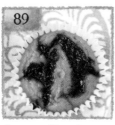

Lemon Raspberry
Swirl Muffins

Vanilla White
Peach Muffins

Biscuits & Gravy

Fluffy Blueberry
Pancakes

Bacon Sweet
Potato Hash with
Apples & Pears

Cinnamon Rolls

Fig Blueberry
Jam

Blackberry
Pear Jam

Starters & Snacks

107
Rosemary
Crackers

109
Sweet Plantain
Guacamole

111
Easy Guacamole

113
Candied Bacon

115
Pulled Pork
Nachos

117
Spinach & Artichoke
Stuffed Portobello
Mushrooms

119
Avocado
Caprese Stacks

121
Prosciutto Pears
with Balsamic
Reduction

123
Citrus Mint
Sugar Salad

Soups & Hearty Salads

127
Sage & Shallot
Delicata Squash
Soup

129
Creamy
Cauliflower Soup

131
Crock-Pot
French Onion
Soup

133
Pumpkin
Tomato Soup

135

Squash Medley
Lavender Soup

137

Chicken
Zoodle Soup

139

Savory Beef Chili

141

Steak Fajita Salad

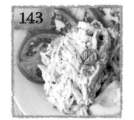

143

Creamy Pesto
Chicken Salad

145

Cranberry
Chicken Salad

Pork Dishes

149

Pan-Seared
Rosemary Sage
Pork Chops with
Apples & Pears

151

Slow Cooker
Pulled Pork

153

Twice-Baked
Stuffed Butternut
Squash

154

Perfect Ribs

157

Shredded Pork
Meatloaf

159

Loaded BBQ
Sweet Potatoes

161

Asian Cabbage
Slaw Pork Burgers

163

Perfect Meatballs
with Sage Sweet
Potato Noodles

Beef Dishes

Sweet & Savory
Open-Faced Sliders

Four-Layer Beef &
Bacon Casserole

Bacon Beef Stew

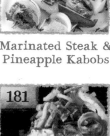
Marinated Steak &
Pineapple Kabobs

Carne Asada

Garlic & Thyme
Standing Rib Roast

Mongolian Beef over
Cauliflower Rice

The Perfect
Burger

Rosemary Sun-Dried
Tomato Meatballs
with Tomato Sauce

Chicken Dishes

Chicken Apricot
Curry

Honey Mustard
Chicken Thighs

Lemon & Chive Pasta
with Chicken Thighs

Lemon Rosemary
Roasted Chicken

Hot Wings

Honey Ginger
Wings

Slow Cooker
Tomatillo Chicken

Spaghetti Squash
Chicken Fritters

Fish & Seafood Dishes

205

Herb Cauliflower
Mash with Seared
Sea Scallops

207

Creamy Seafood
Risotto

209

Shrimp Scampi

211

Honey-Glazed
Salmon with
Pomegranate &
Pineapple Salsa

213

Bacon-Wrapped
Scallop &
Melon Skewers

Sides

217

Honey Dijon &
Rosemary Grilled
Sweet Potatoes

219

Dill Butternut
Squash Fries

221

Bacon Lime
Sweet Potato Salad

223

Grilled
Baby Bok Choy

225

Bacon Pecan
Cabbage

227

Asian Marinated
Asparagus

229

Honey Lime
Roasted Carrots

231

Coconut
Cauliflower
Curry

233

Parsnip Puree

235

Cauliflower Rice

Refreshing Smoothies & Warming Drinks

239
Watermelon
Mint Chiller

241
Afternoon
Pick-Me-Up
(Coffee Smoothie)

243
Hazelnut
Hot Chocolate

245
Cinnamon
Pecan Latte

247
Gingerbread Latte

249
Pineapple
Green Smoothie

251
Banana Berry
Smoothie

253
Ginger Apple Pear
Smoothie

255
Orange Cream
Smoothie

Desserts

259
Coffee Pecan
Ice Cream

261
Blueberry Rosemary
Ice Cream

263
Honey Pistachio
Ice Cream

265
Chocolate Cookie
Ice Cream

267
Macadamia
Chocolate Chip
Cookies

269
Lemon Poppyseed
Cookies

271
No-Bake Tropical
Escape Cookies

273
Gingersnap Pumpkin
Butter Cookie
Sandwiches

275

Candied Bacon
Chocolate Brownies

277

Vanilla Bean
Chocolate-Cayenne
Cake

279

Lime Pound Cake

281

Frozen Blueberry
Cheesecake

283

Black &
White Cake

285

Chocolate Coffee
Bread Pudding

287

Individual
Apple Crisps

Condiments, Nut Butters, & Nut Milks

293

Pistachio Pesto

295

Garlic Aioli

297

Avocado Mousse

299

Pico de Gallo

301

Blueberry
BBQ Sauce

303

Tangy BBQ Sauce

305

Coconut Butter

307

Macadamia
Nut Butter

309

Maple Cinnamon
Pecan Butter

311

Vanilla Bean
Almond Butter

313

Homemade
Nut Milks

INDEX

Acknowledgments

No book is just one person's adventure, and this one in particular has been quite the team effort. We have not just benefited but flourished from so many people's expertise and wisdom.

To Erich, Michele, Holly, and Susan at Victory Belt Publishing: Thank you for helping to bring our vision to life. Your guidance, encouragement, and expertise motivated us to push through the tough times and create something beautiful.

To Hayley and Bill Staley: Thank you for being amazing friends. We could not have asked for anyone better to write the opening words for our labor of love. Your loving and supportive words were always delivered just when needed. You are two amazing people whom we are blessed to call family. We love you two.

To Stacy, Vanessa, Fergie, and friends in California and Colorado: There isn't enough room on this page to list every reason we love you. Your unwavering support whenever we needed dishes done, recipes tasted, or food to eat simply because we couldn't cook anymore is greatly appreciated.

To all our amazing friends in the Paleo community who have set the stage and lit the path for us to follow: We wouldn't be here without all the love and support you have continued to show us. All your amazing websites and cookbooks inspire us daily to continue on this mission to make the world a healthier place.

To our readers: Without you, none of this would be possible. Thank you for reading our websites, making our recipes, and sharing them with your friends and families. Your comments, questions, and encouragement made this book possible—it truly does take a village. Thank you for helping us raise our first book baby.

We have been given countless opportunities to tap into the minds of so many selfless and gifted people in and out of the Paleo world. Each one of you has provided us with so much love and understanding during this journey, and we are eternally grateful. We can only hope that what has resulted from our hard work and your labors of love will not only make you hungry but also help you thrive every day.

Juli would like to thank:

Laura: You've been there for me from day one, and I couldn't be more thankful. Thank you for trying my recipes, helping me set up my props for pictures, and pretty much creating content for my site during my extremely boring moments. You are my best friend and biggest supporter. I would not be here without you.

Brian: You're pretty great. Thank you for sticking with me through the ups and downs. Your support, advice, and laughter are what keep me writing. Thank you for laughing, even when I'm not actually funny.

Peter Schmalfeldt: Without your help with my website, there is absolutely no way I would be here. Thank you for your patience, amazing eye for website design, and ongoing support. I will forever be grateful for what you have done for me.

CrossFit Broadway: I love my gym. I can't say enough about the people and the place that have created such a happy life for me. That gym and the workouts are what keep me on a healthy path, wanting to inspire others in and outside the gym.

Adam from Bodeefit: Thank you for your never-ending support. I am so happy to be part of your amazing company, which can bring fitness, health, and happiness to anyone, anywhere. I look forward to seeing your company grow and thrive.

George would like to thank:

Henneys: Thank you for always being my rock. No matter where in the world I am, I always know your amazing love and support are one phone call away. You have all loved and supported me unconditionally as one of your own, and I am forever grateful. We can all share a laugh in hoping that maybe Trevor will eat some vegetables now.

My grandmother, Georgia: You amaze me every day. Your strength, resolve, and dedication to making others' lives better motivate me every day. I am blessed to always have your unconditional love and support.

My brother: You are the reason I work so hard every day. You are a bright shining light in my life, and I am proud to have you as a brother.

Lindsey: You have helped me experience levels of life I did not know possible. You are a beautiful person, and I am humbled and grateful to have you in my life.

All my family and friends: I want to thank you each individually, but that isn't possible without writing another book. My life is amazing thanks to all your love and support. You have guided me when I was lost, picked me up when I was down, and believed in me when I needed a swift kick in the bottom. I appreciate every one of you seeing my potential and pushing me to achieve it. From the bottom of my heart, I love and appreciate you for making me the best version of myself. This is just the beginning, and I look forward to our future together.

Leah and the E.A.T. Marketplace staff: Thank you for welcoming me as family, feeding Juli and me delicious food when we were tired of cooking for ourselves, and being such a massive force in the real-food movement. Your hard work is changing lives, and it is genuinely appreciated.

Extend the Life of Your Produce!

Here's how.

Green onions need to be placed, unwashed, in a container with a couple inches of water. Cover and store in the refrigerator for up to 1 week.

Peppers need to be stored, dry and unwashed, in a plastic bag with perforations. You can store them in the crisper drawer for up to 5 days.

Cucumbers need to be wrapped, dry and unwashed, in a paper towel and stored in a plastic bag. Store for up to 1 week in the crisper drawer.

Lettuce. When you bring lettuce home, it's best to separate the leaves and wash them in a sink full of cold water. Dry the leaves and then roll them in a clean kitchen towel or paper towels and place in a sealable bag. Keep in an area of the refrigerator where they won't get damaged (tender lettuce is easily crushed by heavier foods and will freeze if kept in a too-cold area of the fridge) and store for up to 1 week.

Summer squash and zucchini. Store dry, unwashed summer squash and zucchini in a plastic bag, removing as much air as possible by wrapping the bag around the squash. Keep the squash in a crisper drawer for up to 5 days.

Asparagus is best stored in water. Without washing the asparagus, cut an inch off the bottom of the stems and place in a container with 2 inches of water. Cover with a plastic bag and store in the refrigerator for up to 5 days.

The Paleo Kitchen

Finding
Primal Joy in
Modern Cooking

JULI BAUER & GEORGE BRYANT

FOOD STORAGE TIPS

REFRIGERATOR

Apples	Cauliflower	Grapes
Beans	Celery	Jalapeños
Berries	Cherries	Leafy greens
Broccoli	Cucumbers	Mushrooms
Cabbage	Eggplants	Zucchini
Carrots	Ginger	

ROOM TEMPERATURE OR COOL PANTRY

Apricots

Avocados

Bananas

Citrus

Garlic

Kiwi

Melons

Nectarines

Onions

Peaches

Pears

Pineapples

Plums

Sweet potatoes

Winter squash

The Paleo Kitchen

Finding
Primal Joy in
Modern Cooking

JULI BAUER & GEORGE BRYANT

A PALEO CHECKLIST

HERE IS A SNAPSHOT OF
WHAT YOU SHOULD BE
EATING ON A DAILY BASIS:

GRASS-FED MEATS

WILD-CAUGHT FISH
AND SEAFOOD

VEGETABLES ← *particularly leafy greens and other low-starch vegetables*

FRUITS

NUTS and SEEDS

HEALTHY FATS/OILS

AND THE FOODS
YOU SHOULD AVOID:

ABSOLUTELY ALL GRAINS

"FAKE FOOD"

REFINED OILS and SUGARS

LEGUMES ← *including corn and soy*

STARCHY VEGETABLES,
PARTICULARLY WHITE
POTATOES*

DAIRY*

ALCOHOL*

all processed foods or foods with long, indecipherable ingredients lists

✳ YOU CAN REINTRODUCE
STARCHY VEGETABLES, DAIRY,
AND ALCOHOL TO YOUR DIET
AFTER THE FIRST THIRTY DAYS
OF THE TRANSITION PERIOD
TO DETERMINE IF YOU HAVE
SENSITIVITIES TO THEM.

The Paleo Kitchen

Finding
Primal Joy in
Modern Cooking

JULI BAUER & GEORGE BRYANT

STICKING TO PALEO

In the past several years that we have been on our Paleo journey, George and I have learned a lot about the challenges of staying on a Paleo diet. But if we had to narrow it down to the top four things that have helped us tremendously in sticking with Paleo, it's these four:

1. CONSISTENCY

The more often you eat Paleo and the more often you cook Paleo meals, the easier it will become to stick with Paleo. Once you become familiar with Paleo ingredient choices—those to eat daily and those to avoid—you'll find it easier to make choices at restaurants because you'll know how to turn a restaurant's offerings into your own Paleo meal. Before you know it, eating Paleo will become second nature.

IN "EATING OUT PALEO STYLE" ON PAGE 66, WE'VE INCLUDED LOTS OF TIPS FOR DINING OUT AND KEEPING TO A PALEO DIET.

2. MODERATION

Remember that just because you are eating something that is Paleo, it doesn't mean that you can eat three times as much. That goes for the cookies, the pancakes, and even the savory foods, like chili. Just as with any healthy diet that has ever been marketed, moderation is key to finding a healthy balance within your body.

3. BALANCE

Just because you have taken on this new lifestyle choice doesn't mean that your friends have, or even that they want to hear about it. So when you head to a potluck or a friend's house and they bring out their famous homemade pizza and chocolate cupcakes, there is no need to be rude. If you are being strict with your diet, explain to them that you won't be able to have any this time around. Or maybe, since it's only once a year that they make this food, have a couple bites (as long as you know it won't bug your stomach too much).

4. EXERCISE

Both of us are huge advocates of exercise. We fully believe everyone should move every day. Whether it's a walk around your neighborhood, weightlifting, spin class, CrossFit, kickboxing, or really anything that keeps your muscles strong, we want you to do it.

Dash

The Paleo Kitchen

Finding
Primal Joy in
Modern Cooking

JULI BAUER & GEORGE BRYANT